D1535124

20TH CENTURY
DEFENDERS OF THE FAITH

20th Century
Defenders of the Faith

Some Theological Fashions Considered
in the Robertson Lectures for 1964

ALEC R. VIDLER

SCM PRESS LTD
BLOOMSBURY STREET LONDON

Also by Alec R. Vidler

CHRISTIAN BELIEF
CHRIST'S STRANGE WORK
WINDSOR SERMONS
ESSAYS IN LIBERALITY
etc.

FIRST PUBLISHED 1965
© SCM PRESS LTD 1965
PRINTED IN GREAT BRITAIN BY
BILLING AND SONS LTD
GUILDFORD AND LONDON

CONTENTS

PREFACE

I wish to thank the University of Glasgow for the honour of being invited to give the Robertson Lectures and for many kindnesses received during my visits there. The title of the book and my frequent references to 'the defence of the Christian religion' derive from the prescribed object of the lectureship.

The lectures are published as they were delivered. If I once started to expand them or to extend their scope, I doubt whether I should be able to come to a finish. As it is, the limits of what I tried to do are, I hope, made sufficiently clear and also the personal standpoint which I adopted. Even so, there are many theologians and tendencies of thought which I find it hard to pardon myself for not having even mentioned. But I fancy there may be many readers who are interested in the recent ferment in theology without being aware that a great deal of this kind of thing has been going on for as long as I can remember, and before that. How far what has been attempted recently is of more intrinsic importance than what was attempted before, or is likely to have more enduring effects, I consider it is as yet too soon to judge.

A.R.V.

King's College
Cambridge
May 1964

I

Liberal Protestantism

IN MY sub-title I do not use the word 'fashions' in a pejorative or derogatory sense. I have been reflecting on the fact that during my lifetime there has been a large variety of types or styles of theological thinking. They have been 'fashions' in the sense that each enjoyed a vogue for a time, until it was more or less superseded by another. I say 'more or less superseded' since some of us continue with a theological, as with a sartorial, fashion when it is no longer in vogue. Many ministers of the Church still affect the Edwardian form of clerical neckwear which in my view has been deservedly superseded! But I am prepared to believe that there are past theological fashions which may not deserve to have been superseded, or which at least deserve to be looked at again and considered and evaluated afresh.

I also intend the word 'fashion' in my title to indicate that I propose to consider an approximately chronological succession of theological styles. It so happens that the beginning of my own life conveniently coincided with the beginning of the present century, and while I did not immediately attain to years of theological discretion—indeed, I am not sure that I have ever done that—I have for long been interested in some of the theological fashions that have been in vogue in my time—not least in those that had held the field just before I became a student, and that had not then found their way into the history books but were still being talked about a lot.

The theological fashions that I have selected for consideration are those in which I happen to have been personally most interested: I am well aware that I shall not be dealing with others in which you may be more interested and may justly rate more highly. I am not attempting to cover anything like the range that Dr Macquarrie covers in his admirable book *Twentieth Century Religious Thought* (1963). Nor am I intending to claim that the theological fashions I am going to look at have been the most important or the most influential in the whole area of what was once Christendom. My selection, I am sure, reflects my own narrow and provincial limitations. For instance—to give only one example of my limitations—I must confess that I have never been interested in thomism or neo-thomism.

Then again, while I have been an interested and grateful admirer of, and debtor to, the work of Scottish theologians, I am not going to speak about them, partly because you will obviously know more about them than I do, and partly because your divines have a kind of philosophical and professional expertness, which always leaves me with a sense of incapacity and inferiority. I am no more than a general practitioner, or perhaps little more than an amateur, in theology. My own cast of mind is historical. Maybe I should add—though this is a terrible confession to make nowadays—it is more spectatorial than engaged. What I mean is that I am interested in what other people have thought, and have never been able to attach much importance to my own thoughts.

DEFENDING RELIGION?

The Robertson Lectures are said to be 'for the defence of the Christian religion', and I ought to say a word or two about that expression. I believe it is not unknown for the defined purpose of courses of lectures, which were endowed some generations ago, to cause a certain embarrassment to those who are invited to deliver them now. In the present instance, I do not myself much care for the expression 'the

Christian religion': it is not an expression that I am in the habit of using except to criticize it. However, I am willing to regard it as an appropriate synonym for what the New Testament calls 'the Gospel of Christ', but then I should have to say that I do not like talk about 'defending' it or suggestions that it needs to be defended or can be satisfactorily defended by mortal men. Luther stated the case here better than I could:

> We tell our Lord God plainly: If he will have his Church, then he must look how to maintain and defend it: for we can neither uphold nor protect it. And well for us, that it is so! For in case we could, or were able to defend it, we should become the proudest asses under heaven. Who is the Church's protector, that hath promised to be with her to the end, and the gates of hell shall not prevail against her? Kings, Diets, Parliaments, Lawyers? Marry no such cattle.[1]

I would add to the list—theologians, and certainly myself!

Nevertheless, I do not want to cavil unreasonably about the terms in which the object of this lectureship is prescribed. It is a fact that theologians have conceived it to be their duty and their office to commend the faith that was in them as persuasively as possible to their contemporaries, and so to exert themselves 'for the defence of the Christian religion', whether or no they put it just like that. So what I aim at doing is to get inside, so far as I can, some of the ways in which the Christian religion has been ostensibly defended— or commended—during my lifetime. In other words, I am going to take another look at some 20th century types of 'Christian apologetic'. It strikes me that there is a tendency nowadays for authors of textbooks and the like to sum them up—to sum up, for example, Liberal Protestantism or Catholic Modernism—in a few stock phrases, to treat them as dated and hopelessly out of court, and fittingly dismissed with an epitaph. My aim—in which I can hardly hope to

[1] *Luther's Table Talk*: see S. T. Coleridge, *On the Constitution of Church and State* (1839 edn.), p. 122.

succeed—is to bring them to life again and to recapture some of the confidence and zest with which they were espoused by those for whom they represented an authentic response to the challenge of their times.

HARNACK ON THE MESSAGE OF JESUS

I begin with Liberal Protestantism. Of the theological fashions—or perhaps 'versions of Christian faith' would be a better way of putting it—which I am going to consider, Liberal Protestantism is the one that has appealed to me least, at any rate until recently. In fact, for so long as I can remember, I have adopted a very negative attitude to it. But now I am wondering whether I have done justice to it. Moreover, I have come to suspect that throughout my lifetime it has done much more than any other version of Christian faith to enable ordinary people—as distinguished from sophisticated theologians—to continue to be professing Christians.

I am going to consider three expositors of Liberal Protestantism in the heyday of its popularity—a German, a Frenchman and an Englishman. The German properly comes first, both because the spade work behind this way of thinking was mostly done in Germany, and because Harnack's *What is Christianity?* is the most renowned manifestation of it. It is interesting that after a long interval, during which I fancy it remained unread, two new editions of the English translation have appeared in recent years.

Rudolf Bultmann says that, whereas between 1900 and 1927 Harnack's book went through fourteen editions in Germany, and exerted an extraordinary influence not only on the rising generation of theologians but also on the educated classes generally, in 1950 few theological students had even read the book. One reason why it should be read, Bultmann says,[1] is that 'the young theologian may . . . learn . . .

[1] In his introduction to Harnack's *What is Christianity?* (Harper Torchbooks, 1957).

from this book . . . what conceptions of Christianity he may presuppose to be current among the broad circles of the educated and semi-educated laymen to whom he must address his sermons and teachings'. I do not know how it may be in Scotland, but I apprehend that would be equally true in England. Bultmann also suggests that Harnack's themes still have plenty of life in them, and are likely to present themselves to theologians with a new vigour, strengthened as it were by their long repose.

Harnack was born in 1851. Both his father and his grand-father had been theologians, so that theology may be said to have been in his blood. But he soon reacted against the ultra-orthodox environment in which he was brought up, and became a Ritschlian, though by no means a blind disciple of Ritschl. He made a rapid ascent in the academic world and from 1889 was a Professor at Berlin. Harnack was a man of encyclopedic learning and a prolific author. But he was also a great public figure, with social prestige and influence. He was a gifted lecturer who could fascinate and enchant his audiences.

His *magnum opus* was the seven-volume *History of Dogma* which was published in German from 1885 to 1888, and translated into English in the following decade. It is still highly valued for the historical information it contains, even by those who disapprove of the Ritschlian axioms which governed Harnack's presentation and interpretation of his material. Thus he supposed that the original gospel which, for him as for Ritschl, centred in the life and teaching of the Jesus of history was soon overlaid by alien elements.

The early Fathers, in attempting to make the gospel intelligible in the Greek world, imposed upon it Greek philosophical and dogmatic theories. And, at the same time, what were originally loosely federated communities of believers became organized into the centralized Great Church with its hierarchy, its laws and discipline, and its sacramental system. Eastern Orthodoxy represented the incursion of

Greek thought, Western Catholicism of Roman organization. So, according to Harnack, living faith was transformed
into a creed, devotion to Christ into christology, the ministers
of the Spirit into clerics, and so on. Like Ritschl he held that
the Reformation had been an only partially successful
attempt to recover the simplicity and freedom of the original
gospel—which had never been entirely extinguished by the
dogmatic systems and the ecclesiastical structures which were
so foreign to it.

It is perhaps important to bear in mind that this massive
historical work lay behind Harnack's popular book *What is
Christianity?* This was a course of sixteen lectures given *ex
tempore* to 600 students drawn from all faculties in Berlin
University in 1899. One of the students, to Harnack's surprise, had taken them all down in shorthand, so he was able
to publish them, and they were soon translated into many
foreign languages. The English translator reports that the
lectures solaced the last days of Queen Victoria's daughter,
the Empress Frederick.

It is commonly said—and I am afraid I used to say this
myself—that in Harnack's view the essence of Christianity
consisted of belief in the Fatherhood of God and the brotherhood of man. But no such vulgar summary can do justice to
the subtlety of this book's theme or to the resourcefulness
and charm with which it is presented. Bare terms like 'the
Fatherhood of God and the brotherhood of man', which
anyhow is not Harnack's own summary of his message, can
sound dreadfully thin. If we are to summarize at all, we
should remember that Harnack said that the teaching of
Jesus could be grouped under three heads : 'The Kingdom of
God and its coming; God the Father and the infinite value
of the human soul; and the higher righteousness and the
commandment of love.'

That Jesus' message is so great and so powerful lies in the fact
that it is so simple and on the other hand so rich; so simple
as to be exhausted in each of the leading thoughts which he

uttered; so rich that every one of these thoughts seems to be inexhaustible and the full meaning of the sayings and parables beyond our reach. But more than that—he himself stands behind everything that he said. His words speak to us across the centuries with the freshness of the present (p. 46).[1]

It is certainly fair to say that, for Harnack, Christianity— he was quite happy with the word 'religion'—was the religion *of* Jesus rather than the religion *about* Jesus. Yet he did not simply identify the Gospel with the religion of Jesus. On the contrary, he said that 'either the Gospel is in all respects identical with its earliest form, in which case it came with its time, and with its time has departed; or else it contains something which, under differing historical forms, is of permanent validity'.

Harnack, like the other Ritschlians, was confident that the teaching and personality of Jesus are plainly communicated through the synoptic gospels. But he did not regard everything in the synoptic gospels as belonging to the essence of Christianity. He distinguished—as I suppose we all do in one way or another—between what was essential and what was accidental, between what was of permanent and what was of transitory validity, or—to use the image of which he was fond—between the kernel and the husk. The kernel of eternal truth never can be expressed in history except in connexion with contingent or temporary modes of thought and perspective.

It is not true, as is sometimes suggested, that Harnack ignored the eschatological or apocalyptic elements in the synoptic account of the teaching of Jesus. He allowed that they were firmly embedded in the records, but in his view they should be understood as part of the husk, which Jesus shared with his contemporaries, and not of the kernel which was original to himself. So Harnack writes:

There can be no doubt about the fact that the idea of the two kingdoms, of God and of the devil, and their conflicts, and

[1] References are to the 5th edition of *What is Christianity?* (1958).

of that last conflict at some future time when the devil, long cast out of heaven, will be also defeated on earth, was an idea which Jesus simply shared with his contemporaries. He did not start it, but he grew up in it and he retained it. The other view, however, that the kingdom of God 'cometh not with observation', that it is already here, was his own (p. 48).

In other words, the kernel of truth was that the kingdom of God is a present possession, the rule of God in the hearts of men : it is identical with eternal life. It is life lived in the conviction that God is our Father, that his providence rules over our whole life and over the world, and that we are his children, of infinite value in his sight, with a divine sonship which is at once a gift to be received and a vocation to be fulfilled.

Thus, according to Harnack, 'the Gospel is no theoretical system of doctrine or philosophy of the universe; it is doctrine only in so far as it proclaims the reality of God the Father. It is a glad message assuring us of life eternal, and telling us what the things and the forces with which we have to do are worth' (p. 110). It is 'eternal life in the midst of time, by the strength and under the eyes of God' (p. 18).

Harnack has no scruples about affirming the individual and subjective character of this experience.

> The kingdom of God comes by coming to the individual, by entering into his soul and laying hold of it. True, the kingdom of God is the rule of God; but it is the rule of the holy God in the hearts of individuals. . . . From this point of view everything that was dramatic in the external and historical sense has vanished; and gone, too, are all the external hopes for the future (pp. 49f.).
>
> Jesus never had anyone but the individual in mind, and the abiding disposition of the heart in love (p. 86).

The subsequent development of the Church obscured and perverted this truth—and how it did so is the subject of the second half of Harnack's lectures which popularize the theme of his *History of Dogma*. It will suffice for me to quote his confident assertion:

> The whole outward and visible institution of a Church *claiming divine dignity* has no foundation whatever in the Gospel. It is a case, not of distortion, but of total perversion. Religion has here strayed away in a direction that is not its own (pp. 184f.).

Evidently, some place is left for a church not claiming divine dignity, for a free fellowship or association of believers. It has, I think, been justly said that the kind of development in Protestant church life which Harnack would have welcomed would be one that pointed more and more 'towards Independentism and the pure community of spirit of the kind represented by the Quakers and by Congregationalism'.[1] Professor William Sanday of Oxford in his fairly sympathetic *Examination of Harnack's What is Christianity?* (1901), commenting on this point, said with regard to the Protestantism of Germany:

> I have no doubt that on the whole side of corporate and external religion the conception that prevails in those circles with which I am best acquainted (the literary and professorial) is defective. It suffers from extreme reaction. Because this side of religion was most liable to abuse and has been most abused in the past, a writer like Harnack does not set to work patiently to correct it, but comes very near to sweeping it away altogether (p. 26).

But, *pace* Dr Sanday, we may be permitted to doubt whether Harnack would have felt differently if he had been more closely acquainted with the ecclesiasticism of Oxford.

However that may be, it must be allowed that, in this as in other respects, the tide of Christian thought and activity has since Harnack's time been flowing in a very different direction. Indeed, three years before his death in 1930 an Englishman is said to have asked a German student: 'What is the

[1] W. Pauck, *Union Seminary Quarterly Review*, March 1958, p. 42.

present position of Harnack?', and the reply given was: 'We have conducted him to Olympus, from which he looks down upon a world which knows him no more.'[1]

Until recently, that seemed to be so, but I have a suspicion that, unlike many divines who have been conducted to Olympus, Harnack is making a come-back, and particularly in regard to what he said about the churchifying of the gospel.

There is one respect, I should say, in which Harnack unnecessarily exposed his position to adverse criticism, for he gave the impression that it was intended to be a *reduced* Christianity. He said, for instance, that 'the whole of Jesus' message may be reduced to these two heads—God as Father, and the human soul so ennobled that it can and does unite with Him' (p. 55); or that at the Reformation 'Religion was taken out of the vast and monstrous fabric which had been previously called by its name . . . and was *reduced* to its essential factors, to the Word of God and to faith' (p. 189). His use of the word 'reduced' made it possible to allege—I have done this myself—that Harnack was proposing an impoverished gospel, a cheapened gospel, only the skeleton of a gospel. Even if in the end something of this kind may be said, it should not be based on his use of the word 'reduced', which after all is a word that can have good implications. If someone speaks of reducing his weight, he expects to be better in health and more vigorous as a result of the process.

RÉVILLE ON THE FUTURE OF CHRISTIANITY

I shall have more to say about Harnack, but I turn now to a French representative of Liberal Protestantism—Jean Réville. He was born in 1854 at Rotterdam where his father, Albert Réville, was pastor to a French-speaking congregation. He graduated in theology at Geneva, and also studied

[1] See A. L. Drummond, *German Protestantism since Luther* (1951), pp. 148f.

at German universities, finally at Paris where he was pastor of a Protestant congregation of highly educated people. His father became a Professor at the Collège de France in 1881. Jean a few years later became editor of the learned journal *Revue d'histoire des religions* and continued to be so till his death. He was also a professor in the Protestant Faculty of Theology in Paris, where he taught patristics and the general history of religions. In 1907 Jean Réville was nominated to the Professorship at the Collège de France which was vacant through the death of his father. But he held it for only a short time, since he died in the following year at the comparatively early age of 53.

In 1902 Réville had given a course of five lectures in Geneva specifically on 'Liberal Protestantism'. They were subsequently published, and translated into Dutch, German and English. For a reason which is obscure, in the English edition (1903) the title was changed from 'Liberal Protestantism' to 'Liberal Christianity', but all the way through the book Réville speaks about Liberal *Protestantism* and Liberal *Protestants*. Though Réville's position is much the same as Harnack's, his writing has a sharper edge and is more precise. If anything, he is even more confident than Harnack that the future belongs to his way of defending the Christian religion.

Réville starts not from the New Testament but from the Reformation. Since he is explicitly writing about 'Liberal Protestantism' and seeking to explain to interested inquirers what it is, he has first to explain how it is both connected with, and different from, the Protestantism of the Reformation. So, in his opening chapter on the 'Genesis of Liberal Protestantism', he maintains that it 'arose out of traditional Protestantism, by virtue of the same causes which, in the 16th century, made the Reformation proceed out of the Catholic Church'. At the Reformation the Bible was primarily appealed to as an historical authority with which to judge the teaching and institutions of the Catholic Church.

It was the consequent controversy with Catholicism that
caused Protestants to treat the Bible not only as an historical
authority but as an infallible authority. Notwithstanding
appearances to the contrary, the pioneers of Protestantism
had stood for the principles of freedom of inquiry and of the
religious supremacy of the individual conscience—although
he granted that they had had no clear understanding of the
true nature or immense import of these principles. Gradually, however, in the following centuries these inherent
principles of the Reformation were unfolded and given their
full weight. Historical criticism and the comparative study
of religions had shattered belief in the infallibility and supernatural inspiration of the Bible. Liberal Protestants welcomed this development. They mean, Réville writes,

> to be freethinkers in the full and true acceptation of the term
> —that is to say, men who think freely, not professed un-
> believers. They mean to be free believers—that is to say, men
> who, in the realm of the moral life and in the vast domain
> beyond the ken of positive science, found their beliefs on free
> enquiry and moral experience (pp. 35f.).

The following three chapters purport to show how Liberal
Protestantism is founded on experience—religious, moral
and social experience. Réville is not at pains—as some later
writers have been—to explain what is meant by 'religious
experience': it is an expression that Harnack also used
occasionally without explanation. Under this heading,
Réville is really making his reckoning with the New
Testament.

True Christianity, he contends, is the religion taught and
lived by Jesus, not that which his followers built around his
person and work. He suggests that the relation between
Jesus and Catholicism is analogous to that between Socrates
and Neo-platonism.

While Réville appears at first sight to allow more than
Harnack did for the difficulty of ascertaining the truth about

the Jesus of history even from the synoptic gospels, yet he states his own conclusions on the subject in an unhesitating manner. Thus on the one hand he writes:

From what is related in the Gospels, it is beyond doubt that Jesus believed in the approaching end of the world as it existed in His day, and in the establishment of the Kingdom of God on earth in the near future; it is beyond doubt that He admitted the existence of demons, and that when He effected the cure of sick people He believed He was driving these demons from the bodies of their victims. It is certain that Jesus shared in the ideas current among the Jews of His day regarding the place of the earth in the universe and the respective positions of the earth and the heavens. We no longer hold these ideas. . . . There is not a single person to-day, even among those Christians who think themselves most strictly bound to the literal teaching of the Bible, who entertains on all these questions the same notions as Jesus and His apostles (p. 51f.).

At the same time, Réville is equally confident that 'the value of the religious and moral teaching of Jesus for us is independent of the local and temporary forms in which it was embodied' (p. 53). And here is his account of the religious and moral teaching of Jesus:

Jesus came to invite men, all men, of every class, race and creed, to enter into the Kingdom of God. He bid them repent and cultivate a lively feeling of their wretchedness and faults, not indeed in order to lose themselves in despairing revolt, nor to sink beneath the feeling of their native and fatal powerlessness, but in order, on the contrary, that the consciousness of their many wants might give rise in their hearts to an ardent desire for restoration, to an intense longing for release, and a better, juster, purer, happier, holier life, and that they might gain the divine forgiveness through this renewing of their being. He also opened out to them the inexhaustible treasures of love for the Heavenly Father and of love for their brethren, saying to them: Come unto Me, prove the benefits which I bring you; do the will of your Father who is in Heaven and who speaks to you, not in the thunder of Sinai and the oracles of the sanctuary, but through the consciences of men, of prophets, of the Son of Man, of the best and holiest of His children, in the only living sanctuary, that is, in your own heart, in the inmost depths of your soul. Be just, for God's law is justice; be good, for goodness is the earth's greatest treasure; be merciful, love one another, for love is the source of life; sacrifice yourselves one for another, for happiness lies in mutual sacrifice, in solidarity; aspire to become perfect, even as your Father in Heaven is perfect (pp. 57f.).

This teaching, Réville says, can be and has been embraced by all sorts and conditions of people, simple and learned. It leaves on one side 'the formidable problems of metaphysical theology (which) greatly exceed the capacity of the human mind' (pp. 62f.). 'Religion', he says,

teaches us nothing either about God's nature or our own; it is compatible with different views of God and man; it is essentially a principle of life, the feeling of *a living relation between the human individual and the powers or power of which the universe is the manifestation* (p. 64).

That is his definition of religion in general. The *Christian* religion he defines as follows:

What has remained, what now remains as the true substance of Christ's Gospel, is what was for Him, before all else, religion, apart from doctrine and ethics, apart from sacraments and institutions, namely, *God, as the Heavenly Father, whatever may be the philosophical description of the Divine Being; men, as the sons of God, and therefore all brethren, whatever the philosophical notion of man's nature; that is what the Gospel has long since taught us to regard as its essence; it is the sovereign affirmation: 'Thou shalt love the Lord thy God with all thy heart, with all thy soul, with all thy mind; thou shalt love thy neighbour as thyself.' And these two commandments are one and the same* (pp. 70f.).

Réville shows himself to be sensitive to the charge that this is a *reduced* Christianity, in a way that Harnack had not been. Liberal Protestantism, he says, has often been upbraided with professing a Christianity reduced, diminished, and, so to speak, emptied of its contents. He replies that those who regard it as 'devoid of contents and poor in spirituality are inflicting a gratuitous injury to the Gospel of Christ, seeing Jesus Himself summed up His preaching on this purely religious and ethical profession' (p. 72). Only let those who speak of its being a poor and reduced religion try to realize it, and then they will know what to think of its alleged inadequacy.

In some respects Réville's Liberal Protestantism appeared to be more reduced than Harnack's. Harnack, while rejecting the christological dogma, had in his own way affirmed the unique divine Sonship of Jesus. He had written : 'How he came to this consciousness of the unique character of his relation to God as a Son; how he came to the consciousness of his power, and to the consciousness of the obligation and the mission which this power carries with it, is his secret, and no psychology will ever fathom it' (p. 98). Réville hardly goes so far as this. Liberal Protestants, he writes,

> venerate Jesus as the greatest of all prophets, the purest and holiest conscience whose memory has been preserved by history, as the one in whom moral truth was most completely manifested in a human soul, the one who, throughout His ministry as Messianic reformer—in so far as we can gather— was the living commentary of His Gospel, and who crowned His work by a sacrifice of such perfect moral sublimity that it has become the type and inspiration of countless sacrifices, proceeding from the same obedience to moral truth (p. 114).

On the other hand, Réville writes more positively and strongly than Harnack about the future of the Churches. Liberal Protestantism, he says, believes

> in the mission of the liberalised Churches in the modern world, for worship, instruction, and education, for healthy and free moral propaganda, for the continual stimulation of works

of solidarity and charity; and it believes that, far from lessening their influence for good, an ever-increasing application of their activity to moral, social, and fraternal works, irrespective of all sacerdotal and dogmatic considerations, opens up a new future, rich in blessings, both for themselves and for society in general (p. 146).

CAMPBELL'S 'NEW THEOLOGY'

I turn now to an English representative of Liberal Protestantism, who was at the time the best-known English representative, though, for reasons which we shall see, his fame as such did not endure. I mean Reginald John Campbell who was Minister of the City Temple in London which, I suppose, might be described as the Mecca, or perhaps as the metropolitan cathedral, of English nonconformity.

Campbell claimed to be Scottish in origin, but he was born in England in 1867, his father being a minister in the United Methodist Church. He was however brought up, until his 'teens, by his maternal grandparents in Northern Ireland, and the earliest religious impressions made on him were those of Ulster Presbyterianism—a very different proposition from English nonconformity, as he was to discover in due course. Campbell's health always seems to have been frail, though in the event he lived to a good old age—he died as recently as in 1956, at the age of 89. He was endowed with an acute intelligence and was always an omnivorous reader.

At Oxford, for reasons of health, he did not distinguish himself as he was expected to do. While he was there, he fell under the influence of Charles Gore and the *Lux Mundi* school of high anglicans. He had previously become a member of the Church of England when teaching for a time in a church school. His intention was to take orders in the Church of England, but he abandoned it because he could not stomach the high anglican theory which unchurched the non-episcopal communions.

He therefore decided to enter the nonconformist ministry,

and was at once—in 1895—appointed to the charge of a more or less derelict downtown congregational chapel in Brighton. Here his extraordinary powers as a preacher at once became manifest, and his congregation rapidly increased and soon outgrew its existing building. *The Times* newspaper in its obituary of Campbell, speaking of this period, said:

> His success was instantaneous, and soon a larger building was secured. To a striking personal appearance—his refined and delicate face was even then crowned by snow-white hair—he added no sensational attitudes or pulpit mannerisms. He preached the great themes of evangelical religion, and his hearers felt that his sympathy responded to their needs.

He may indeed have preached 'the great themes of evangelical religion' but he did so without the standard vocabulary and the stock formulas.

However, he was in Brighton for only a few years, since in 1902 he was called to succeed Dr Parker at the City Temple. The days of great preachers and great preaching were running out, but Campbell quickly became London's most famous, and also most controversial, preacher. He preached his own distinctive form of Liberal Protestantism which came to be known as 'the New Theology'. Three sermons a week were demanded of him and they were all regularly published, so that his teaching reached a far wider circle than could sit under him at the City Temple.

Campbell was sensitive to changes in the intellectual climate, and had a gift for assimilating new ideas and then popularizing them. Thus he was influenced by the neo-Hegelian or English idealist philosophers. He was also a keen and widely read student of biblical criticism and abreast of all the latest theories in that field, too ready perhaps to promulgate them as the last word, before there had been time for them to be digested. Naturally, he read Harnack among the rest, though Harnack appealed to him less than the French Liberal Protestants, Auguste Sabatier[1] and Jean Réville. He was also alert to the work of the Roman Catholic modernists or some of them, whose 'duel with the Vatican', as it has been called, was at this time reaching its crisis.

Out of these and other influences Campbell compounded his 'new theology'. It was bolder, more comprehensive and more daring in speculation than the Liberal Protestantism of Harnack or Réville—though with them he regarded himself as one of a widespread company who had the future of theology in their hands. In his *The New Theology* he wrote:

> It can hardly be denied that in its main bearing, to say no more, it is seen to be rising spontaneously in every part of the civilized world (p. 259).

> The New Theology . . . is primarily a moral and spiritual movement. It is one symptom of a great religious awakening which in the end will reinspire civilization with a living faith in God and the spiritual meaning of life (p. 263).

Campbell's preaching by this time was alarming the more conservative or official elements in English nonconformity, with whom his relations became increasingly strained. It had also become a matter of public controversy in the newspapers and the periodical press. It was these circumstances that led him in 1906 to publish his book, which was a systematic account of the teaching he had been giving at the City Temple. It became a best seller.

It has been said that 'there was little intellectual weight in' the book, and that 'its rather loose statements were easily refuted by Bishop Gore and others' (*The Times*, 2 March 1956). Bishop Gore published a rejoinder, entitled *The New Theology and the Old Religion*, in the following year. It is true that Campbell himself later disowned and withdrew his book. But in my opinion it should not be so lightly

---

[1] See his *Outlines of a Philisophy of Religion based on Psychology and History* (new edn., 1957).

evaluated. It is by no means a mere *réchauffé* of other people's Liberal Protestantism. It is an independently conceived species of the genus. I should say that Campbell's defence of the Christian religion was more ambitious and thorough than Harnack's or Réville's.

They eschewed philosophical or metaphysical questions and what has been known as natural or rational theology—opining that such questions are beyond the capacity of the human mind to answer—and contenting themselves with advocating the following of the religious and moral teaching of Jesus. And Campbell could echo their words as when he wrote:

> Creeds or no creeds, we hold that the religious experience which came to mankind in Jesus of Nazareth is enough for all our needs, and only requires to be freed from limiting statements in order to lay firm hold once more upon the civilized world (p. 4).

But he went much further than they did and made a valiant attempt to grasp nettles which they passed by—even if he did so with too simple a confidence.

So he asks:

> Why is there a universe at all? Why has the unlimited become limited? What was the need for the long cosmic struggle, the ignorance and pain, the apparently prodigal waste of life and beauty? Why does a perfect form appear, only to be shattered and superseded by another? What can it all mean—if, indeed, it has a meaning? (p. 22).

The answers he gives are, as I have indicated, largely inspired by idealist or neo-Hegelian concepts, though he applies them to theological themes with much resourcefulness and ingenuity. His 'New Theology' is not intellectually contemptible, unless Hegel and Hegelianism are held to be so. Campbell, I may say, was also alive to the new psychology, which really was new then, and he draws on the theory of the subconscious. 'Our ordinary consciousness', he writes, 'is but a tiny corner of our personality' (p. 30).

He also went beyond Harnack and Réville in that he had a christology—a doctrine of the eternal Christ—though at the same time he was absolutely firm in his dependence on, and devotion to, the historic Jesus—unlike some of his fellow 'new theologians' like Dr Anderson of Dundee who accepted the Christ-myth theory of Dr Drews. Campbell, on the other hand, did adopt the theory of the Eternal Divine Man, which was then enjoying a vogue, and he worked it into his christology. He did not deny divine transcendence, but he did say 'it is the immanent God with whom we have to do' (p. 5).

In some respects Campbell was surprisingly conservative. He did not adopt a negative attitude to traditional creeds and dogmas—he was no Ritschlian—he claimed to be able to use and interpret them aright. While about the Virgin Birth he was not merely agnostic but emphatically denied that it was an historic fact, on the other hand he accepted the tradition of the physical resurrection of Jesus.

This may suggest that Campbell was a carefree eclectic, but there was a real, if inchoate, coherence in his New Theology. It was bound up too with a social gospel, for Campbell was in close sympathy with the Labour movement. He was a typical Liberal Protestant in regarding the Kingdom of God as primarily intended to be gradually realized in a regenerated human society in the course of history. 'Slowly, very slowly,' he writes, 'with every now and then a depressing set-back, the race is climbing the steep ascent towards the ideal of universal brotherhood' (p. 63).

Unfortunately, Campbell was too reckless in using expressions such as 'the fundamental identity of God and man' (p. 40) which he can hardly have properly weighed, and which, though they were qualified elsewhere, gave easy handles to his critics.

He came to regret that he had ever published his book *The New Theology*, and not only on this account. By 1915 he had changed his mind and come to acknowledge that the criticism of Bishop Gore, which was from a Liberal Catholic point of view, had been justified. He also felt the impact of Schweitzer's attack on the Jesus of Liberal Protestantism and he had been impressed by Fr Tyrrell's book *Christianity at the Cross Roads* and by von Hügel's *The Mystical Element in Religion*. There had always been a strongly mystical strain in Campbell's Liberal Protestantism and he had a hankering after sacramentalism. It was under these impulses that he returned to the Church of England and was reordained. He spent the rest of his life inconspicuously in the anglican ministry, and in a rather wooden high anglican position. He never again cast the old spell as a preacher : *The Times* obituary, perhaps a little unkindly, said that now 'to many thoughtful people many of his sermons seemed little but a succession of commonplaces though charmingly delivered'.

A REPLY

Campbell naturally received plenty of abuse during his 'New Theology' period. If he had not been a Congregationalist with a loyal and devoted congregation, I suppose he might have been the object of a formal heresy hunt. In 1907, the year after the publication of *The New Theology*, a dozen or so of the leaders of English Congregationalism published a volume of sermons and essays, entitled *The Old Faith and the New Theology: a series of sermons and essays on some of the truths held by Evangelical Christians, and the difficulties of accepting much of what is called the 'New Theology'*. As the subtitle implies, this was a temperate work, which made little direct reference to Campbell and was quite free from personal abuse. The object of the exercise was no doubt to reassure Congregationalists who were disturbed by what was being disseminated from the City

Temple. The book contains what may be described as sound and solid expositions of evangelical doctrine. But it does not strike fire, and, so far as lucidity, forthrightness and grace of style go, compares poorly with Campbell's writing. I am not surprised that the pages of the copy which I took out of the Cambridge University library, and which had been there for well over fifty years, had never been cut.

Even the essay by P. T. Forsyth, of whom I expected better things, is disappointing. His subject was 'Immanence and Incarnation'. What was needed was some clear and judicious discussion of these ideas with reference to what the New Theology appeared to be saying, but instead Forsyth indulges the taste for turgid and rhetorical writing which too often beset him. The idea of divine immanence, he says —which had had the wholesome effect of correcting a distant deism, now 'promotes a theosophic mysticism detached from positive faith. . . . It loses redemption in evolution.' The Gospel of grace is one not of emergence but of invasion. 'The mere doctrine of immanence reduces God's action from a historic *moral act* of universal effect to a *cosmic process* extending into the moral world, and, in so far as it is process, destroying ethic' (p. 55f.). And Forsyth went on to say :

> The present conflict in the Church is more critical for Christianity than any that has arisen since the second century. The issue in the Reformation was small beside this. What is at stake is the whole historical character of Christianity. And what is substituted is an ideal Christianity (p. 57).

The parallel between second-century Gnosticism and the New Theology was extremely close, and so on.

I do not think Forsyth made much impression on Campbell. To do so he would have had to engage more closely with what Campbell had actually said and also to enter more sympathetically into the situation which the New Theology was trying to meet.

The New Theology and the Liberal Protestantism of the first decade of this century doubtless had many defects, but it measured the challenge of the times more adequately than the moderating guardians of orthodoxy did.

2

Roman Catholic Modernism

IT IS not my intention to give a conspectus of the whole modernist movement in the Roman Catholic Church. I tried to do that in my book *The Modernist Movement in the Roman Church* (1934). Here and now I want to consider only certain manifestations of it which could be accounted a theological fashion at the beginning of this century: and in particular those manifestations of it which were in the form of a criticism of Liberal Protestantism and which proffered an alternative way—indeed an opposite way—of defending the Christian religion under modern conditions. But some introduction is needed in order that we may see how it came about that in the Roman Catholic Church, which in the 19th century had resisted and repelled every kind of doctrinal innovation, so radical a departure could even have been attempted.

THE BEGINNINGS

It is true that during the 19th century there had been some groups of Roman Catholics who had sought to acclimatize their faith in the modern world. For example, Lamennais and his collaborators in the *Avenir* had made it their ambition to persuade the Church to come to terms with democracy and liberal political régimes.[1] Dr Döllinger and his colleagues at Munich had undertaken to deal with the history of the Church in the light of critical standards of scholarship. Lord Acton and the group associated with him

[1] See my study of Lamennais, *Prophecy and Papacy* (1954).

in the *Rambler* and the *Home and Foreign Review* had embarked on a notable renovation of Catholic literary and scientific culture.[1]

But these and all other essays in liberal Catholicism, as they may be broadly described, had had to be abandoned. The papacy would have none of them. Lamennais and Döllinger left the Church and died excommunicate: Acton had to shut up as a defender of Catholicism. Pius IX's *Syllabus errorum* of 1864 had been only the most conspicuous assertion of the papal attitude to the modern world. When in 1870, after the promulgation of the Vatican decrees, Rome and the States of the Church had been incorporated in the Kingdom of Italy, and the pope became the self-styled Prisoner in the Vatican, that was an eloquent symbol of the papacy's *non possumus* reaction to the modern world and of its determination to hold out to the last in the only citadel remaining to it, with its surviving forces securely disciplined. That is what defending the Christian religion meant to the Roman Church.

If, when Pio Nono died in 1878, he had been succeeded by an equally reactionary pope, no one would have thought it worth while to launch any further essays in liberal Catholicism. A year or two before, one French bishop had written to another:

> May God protect us and save his Church. Pius IX will give his name to this pontificate which is unique not only on account of its length, but on account of the disasters which he has been unable to prevent or perhaps to foresee. Everything that could be lost has been lost: what remains, and what cannot perish, has been compromised. Pius IX is the Louis XVI of the Papacy. He has let himself be driven by events which put everything in jeopardy.[2]

The celebrated French preacher Père Didon says that when he went to Rome for the funeral of Pius IX, grass was grow-

---

[1] See *The Liberal Catholic Movement in England 1848-1864* by J. F. Altholz (1962).   [2] G. Bazin, *Vie de Mgr Maret*, iii. 329.

B

ing high in the piazza of St Peter's: that symbolized the low, indeed the ruinous, condition in which Pio Nono left the Holy See.[1]

We must not exaggerate the difference between Leo XIII and Pius IX. Leo continued to be the protesting Prisoner in the Vatican, and he had no intention of introducing any fundamental changes in the Church. But he did mean to give the Church a new look. He was a great diplomat, and by temperament an optimist. Instead of emphasizing the alienation between the Church and the modern world, he wanted to convince the modern world that it needed the Church and that the Church was no longer sadly aspiring after a restoration of the *ancien régime*.

So, for example, he directed the French Catholics to abandon their quite unrealistic royalism and to rally to the republican constitution of their country. Again, his encyclical *Rerum novarum* was intended to show that the Church did not acquiesce in *laissez faire* capitalism and had a social doctrine suited to the age of industrialism. These measures did not of course affect Catholic dogma. But it seemed as if Leo also wanted to encourage an intellectual revival in the Church. His opening of the Vatican archives to historians was thought to be a sign of this, as was also his making Newman a cardinal, for the Roman curia had viewed him with grave suspicion as long as Pio Nono lived.

These and other measures produced a new and more sanguine atmosphere in the Church. Perhaps, after all, the Church was not irrevocably wedded to living in the past. Perhaps a reconciliation between the Church and modern societies and modern culture was worth taking in hand, and efforts in that direction might be tolerated, if not officially endorsed. It was this impalpable new atmosphere—unsubstantial and precarious as it eventually turned out to be—that created the conditions in which what came to be known as the modernist movement took its rise.

[1] *The Tablet*, 27 April 1963.

THE CRISIS

This movement had many sides and contained many disparate elements. It was a case of a variety of more or less independent initiatives. Thus, there was 'social' modernism[1] —groups of Christian democrats, especially in France and Italy, who, as it were, took up again the task that Lamennais had been compelled to abandon and which had had a brief but quickly blighted second flowering at the time of the 1848 Revolution in France. On the intellectual or theological side, there were attempts to give a new orientation to Catholic philosophy and to break away from the bondage of the rigid scholastic or thomistic orthodoxy which, it had to be confessed, Leo XIII appeared to have canonized in his encyclical *Aeterni Patris* of 1879. There was the lay Catholic philosopher, Maurice Blondel (1861-1949), who propounded a philosophy of 'action' which was based on an analysis of the spiritual life and followed what was known as 'the method of immanence': it was anti-intellectualist if judged by the standards of the theological schools. Blondel's writing was obscure but it certainly represented a new departure. Loosely associated with him was the Oratorian priest, Lucien Laberthonnière (1860-1932); two of his books were put on the Index in 1906 and he was not allowed to publish anything more during his lifetime. Then there was Édouard Le Roy (1870-1954), another lay professor who eventually became a member of the Académie Française: his thought had a good deal in common with the pragmatism of William James and the intuitionism of Henri Bergson, especially the latter. His book *Dogme et Critique* was put on the Index in 1907. These were all philosophical modernists.

Even more striking was the work of a new generation of Catholic biblical scholars, of whom the most eminent and enterprising was Alfred Loisy (1857-1940). They were moved by the need for an all-round renovation of Catholic teaching

[1] See my book *A Century of Social Catholicism 1820-1920* (1964).

about the Bible and for a full utilization of critical methods of study, so that Catholic biblical scholars might be able to hold up their heads alongside Protestant scholars and alongside rationalists in the tradition of Renan. Other modernists attacked the extreme authoritarianism of the Church's discipline and the centralization of power in the Vatican bureaucracy. Father George Tyrrell (1861-1909) became the most prominent spokesman of this form of modernism, though he had plenty of other strings to his bow as well.

These various modernist or modernizing initiatives had scarcely got under way in the latter years of Leo XIII when he was succeeded by Pius X—who did not take the name 'Pius' for nothing. He stood for a reversion to the conservative intransigence of Pius IX. He regarded it as his mission to stamp out all dangerous thinking in the Church, and he had the power to do so. The leading modernists were excommunicated or silenced or compelled to submit. Sympathizers with the movement were tracked down and disciplined. An anti-modernist oath was imposed on all clerics. Even scholars like Batiffol and Lagrange, who had been careful to dissociate themselves from the modernists, were penalized and frustrated in their work. It is hardly an exaggeration to say that a reign of doctrinal terror was maintained until the death of Pius X in 1914, and even then was only gradually relaxed.

In consequence, a promising renaissance of Catholic scholarship, especially biblical scholarship, was set back for more than a generation. I will give one illustration of this which I came across among the von Hügel papers in the library of St Andrews University. Abbot Cuthbert Butler was the distinguished historian of the Vatican Council and the biographer of Archbishop Ullathorne. In 1922 von Hügel told him he wished he would do some work in the field of Christian origins. Butler replied as follows:

In regard to what you say about your regret that I am not giving myself up to early Christian things,—years ago I recognized that these things—Xtian origins, New Testament, History of Dogma, etc.—have been made impossible for a priest, except on the most narrow apologetic lines. A priest can publish nothing without 'imprimatur'. The only freedom in Biblical things and the rest is that of a tram, to go ahead as fast as you like on rails, but if you try to arrive at any station not on the line, you are derailed. Textual criticism of the most technical kind is the only form of biblical study open. . . . When the Biblical Commission got under way, and the Lamentabili and Pascendi were issued, I deliberately turned away from all this work.

The well-known ecclesiastical historian Louis Duchesne had done the same and for the same reason at an even earlier stage, and so had avoided becoming directly embroiled in the modernist movement.

This setback for Catholic scholarship, especially for the critical and objective study of Christian origins, was then one consequence of the nipping in the bud of the modernist movement and of its ruthless suppression.

Another consequence was that the work of the modernists themselves remained inchoate. Conditions did not exist in which they could peaceably develop it, nor in which it could be dispassionately considered and assessed. It became at once enveloped in bitter controversy and clouded by the kind of misrepresentation that seems inevitably to attend upon theological controversy. The modernists, I say, were not free to develop their ideas. Those who remained in the Church were silenced. Others like M. Loisy accepted excommunication as a sign that the cause was lost, and felt themselves to have been discharged from the task of defending the Christian religion. Father Tyrrell, who might have led a continuing revolt, died in 1909. His friend and literary executor, Miss Maude Petre, maintained a lonely witness, and was subjected to ecclesiastical discipline for her loyalty to his memory. Thus the ways of defending the Christian religion which had been adumbrated by the modernists did not receive the consideration that I believe they deserved, and it is only recently that there has been a revival of interest in their work.

LOISY ON THE GOSPEL AND THE CHURCH

It is possible here to look at only three of these modernist essays in the defence of the Christian religion, and it is natural to begin with M. Loisy's book *L'Évangile et l'Église*, since that was a kind of counter-manifesto to Harnack's *What is Christianity?* Fr Tyrrell described *L'Évangile et l'Église* as 'the classical exposition of Catholic Modernism',[1] and it probably is the most important literary product of the movement. But I should myself say that the movement never attained sufficient coherence or unity, or had sufficient enduring influence, to be susceptible of 'a classical exposition'.

A few words about Loisy himself. Born in 1857 in the Champagne country, son of a small farmer, his unusual intelligence was spotted at school and he was sent to college. It was not because of any pressure on the part of his family but out of his own disposition that he became a candidate for the priesthood and had a seminary training. There too his intellectual ability as well as his piety was remarked upon, and he was sent for further training to the Institut Catholique, i.e. the Catholic University, in Paris. Here he was encouraged by Professor Louis Duchesne, and in due course Loisy himself became a professor there, dedicated to biblical and oriental studies.

It should be realized that, though Loisy was a great savant, he was also a devout priest with a keen pastoral sense. He could have pursued a purely academic career, and built up a safe and solid reputation as a semitic philologist, or what have you. What impelled him to become a modernist (though the term had not then been invented) was his devotion to the Church (i.e. to the Roman Catholic Church), his sense of what it ought to be doing for the spiritual and

[1] *Christianity at the Cross Roads* (1963 edn.), p. 76.

moral needs of mankind, and at the same time his realization that it was dreadfully handicapped in its mission to educated people by the backwardness of its theology.

He quickly became an accomplished biblical critic and began to publish the fruits of his studies. It was an asset to him throughout his career, and an annoyance to his opponents, that he was a brilliant writer of French prose with a wicked wit and a delicate irony. He was soon in trouble with the ecclesiastical authorities and was dismissed from his professorship in 1893. However, he now had more time for thought, and it was during the ensuing years that he worked out an apologia for Catholicism—stimulated by his friend Baron von Hügel, and with some help from Newman's *Essay on the Development of Doctrine*. This material was available to him when he came to write *L'Évangile et l'Église*.

It would be a mistake to suppose that he simply made use of the publication of Harnack's popular lectures as an excuse or occasion for producing his own defence of Catholicism or as a peg on which to hang it. Far from it. He sincerely believed that Harnack's thesis cried out to be refuted, and long after Loisy had had, perforce, to abandon the constructive theme of his own book he still adhered to his criticism of Liberal Protestantism.

On the other hand, at the time of its publication (1902) *L'Évangile et l'Église* certainly had a more positive object as well. Describing in retrospect what his aim had been, Loisy wrote:

L'Évangile et l'Église was not exactly what it appeared to be. It was not simply a defence of Catholicism against the criticisms of Liberal Protestantism. There exists an official Catholicism, intransigent, registered in the formularies of the later councils and papal encyclicals, incarnate in the Roman curia, a great political machine by which the papacy manages the business of religion. It was not by any means the author's intention to establish the legitimacy of that Catholicism.

Rather, he intended discreetly to indicate its defects and its dangers. Or better say that the twofold object he had in view was tactfully to instruct the Catholic clergy about the real situation of the problem of Christian origins, while at the same time demonstrating against Protestant criticism that this situation was far from making a defence of Catholicism impossible—, that, on the contrary, the Church could now be seen as a necessary and legitimate development of the Gospel; and that what was rationally untenable was the position of Liberal Protestantism with its supposed essence of Christianity which had been rediscovered only in our own time, after having been lost for more than eighteen centuries.[1]

Harnack had claimed in his book *What is Christianity?* to be dealing with the subject not as a theologian but as an historian. Loisy took him to task on this score. If an historian wants to know what Christianity is he should view it as a whole in its long and complex history and in its total development, whereas what Harnack had done, Loisy claimed, was to select one particular idea, which was congenial to him, in the teaching of Jesus—namely, trust in God as Father —and to treat that as the essence of Christianity, ruling out everything else as unessential. What should we think, he asked, of anyone who selected one particular idea that appealed to him in the teaching of Mohammed, and insisted that that was the essence of Islam without respect to what Mohammed himself and his followers had understood their religion to be?

Harnack, by identifying Christianity with a single, timeless idea, had failed to realize that a religion is a living, growing, dynamic movement which gradually unfolds its meaning, and does not necessarily disclose its essence at its origin. An oak tree is more than an acorn, though there is organic continuity between them. A religion must be looked at as a whole and, even so, as an unfinished whole. In the case of Christianity, it is a mistake to try to isolate within

[1] Introd. to 5th edition.

it an original immutable essence and to contrast that with the developed and still developing tradition and life of the Church in which the religion has revealed itself in the course of history and in its expansion throughout the world.

But Loisy carried his criticism of Harnack further than this. He challenged his interpretation of the original gospel of Jesus. If we study the documents in the light of critical knowledge—and Loisy had some acute objections to make to Harnack's use and assessment of the sources—we do not find that Jesus was above all concerned to instil individual and subjective trust in the divine fatherhood. What he proclaimed was the coming of the eschatological kingdom of God as an objective and social reality, and his own role as the Messiah was central to his gospel. Harnack was mistaken in saying that the original gospel was about the Father and not about the Son. The texts on which he depended for his view had the misfortune to be of doubtful authenticity and of uncertain meaning. For example, Loisy said, if the saying in St Luke's gospel that the Kingdom of God is *entos humōn* (17. 21) 'was really uttered by Jesus and addressed to the Pharisees, as the evangelist says, it cannot have meant that the kingdom of God was *in* them, that is to say, in their souls (which is what Harnack took it to mean); for these Pharisees did not believe in the gospel and had no part at all in the kingdom' (p. 53).[1] The historian, Loisy added, 'must resist the temptation to modernize the idea of the kingdom. The theologian has a right to interpret it so as to adapt it to the conditions of the present time, but he must not confuse his commentary with the primitive sense of the evangelical texts' (p. 54). The kingdom which Jesus proclaimed was not to be realized as a result of a long and slow progress, but it was to come shortly by the act of God.

As regards Jesus himself, the title 'son of God' meant that he was the Messiah who was to inaugurate the kingdom and not merely that he had a unique knowledge of the Father.

[1] References are to the 5th French edition, Paris, 1929.

Harnack's distinction between the kernel and the husk was misconceived. 'It is his own religion,' Loisy wrote, 'not that of the gospel, that M. Harnack expounds and defends when he asserts that "God and the soul, the soul and its God, are the whole contents of the gospel." The historical gospel does not have this mystical and individualistic colour' (p. 92). And again, 'the full life of the gospel does not lie in one element only in the teaching of Jesus, but in the totality of his manifestation which has its point of departure in the personal ministry of the Christ, and its development in the history of Christianity' (p. 99).

The ideas of the kingdom and of the Messiah were the indispensable form in which Christianity had to be born in Judaism before spreading out into the world. Christianity was born of the incomparable teaching and action of Jesus who gathered together and vivified the best of the religious capital that had been accumulated before him by Israel. He transmitted this capital not as a simple deposit which the believers of all ages had only to preserve, but as a living faith which was to live and grow after him through the prevailing influence of the spirit.

Loisy then proceeds to develop his thesis that the ideas of the kingdom and the Messiah, which were rooted in Judaism, had to be transformed into those of the Catholic Church and the incarnate Logos if the gospel was to bring its beneficent influence to bear on the Gentile world. 'Jesus announced the kingdom, and it was the Church that came. It came enlarging the form of the gospel, which it was impossible to keep just as it was, once the ministry of Jesus had been closed by the passion. There is no institution on earth nor in human history, whose legitimacy and value could not be contested, if it be laid down as a principle that nothing has a right to exist except what was in its original condition. This principle is contrary to the law of life, which is a movement and a continual effort of adaptation to perpetually changing and new conditions. Christianity could not escape this law, and it is not to be blamed for having submitted to it. It could not do otherwise' (pp. 153f.).

You do not assure the identity of an individual by making him return to his cradle. 'The Church of today', Loisy writes, 'resembles, no more and no less, the community of the first disciples than an adult man resembles the infant which he was at first' (p. 158).

In the rest of his book Loisy seeks to show how the growth of the Church as an historical institution with its hierarchical structure and its discipline, with its dogma and its cultus, was the legitimate outcome of the original gospel and the means by which it became a religion available for mankind in general, which it could not have done if it had been tied to its primitive form. 'That the Catholic Church', he writes, 'has adapted the gospel and is adapting it still, that it adapts itself continually to the needs of new times, is by no means evidence that it forgets the gospel or slights its own tradition, but that it wants to make both prevail, that it realizes they are flexible and always perfectible' (p. 166).

Thus hellenization, so far from being a corruption of the gospel as Harnack held, was indispensable if Christianity were not to remain a Jewish sect. The faith was not, however, turned by the Greek fathers into a logically consistent philosophical system. The Church was faithful to the data of Christian experience, and did not hesitate to hold together beliefs that seemed to be contradictory as in the dogmas of the incarnation and of grace.

On these lines Loisy found a justification for the Roman Catholic Church of his own time. It will appear to most readers now that he justified too much, including beliefs and practices which Roman Catholics themselves are nowadays submitting to criticism and seeking to reform. But it must be remembered that, if Loisy was to secure acceptance in the Church for his radically novel attempt to relate contemporary Catholicism to the new historical knowledge about Christian origins, he had to proceed tactfully.

Even so, he did not simply defend the *status quo*, but suggested at various points the need for reform and for further development. For example, he suggested that the exaggerated authoritarianism of post-Tridentine Catholicism, and its subordination of the rights of the individual, had been due to reaction against Protestantism, and could be corrected. Again, he said that the Vatican decrees of 1870 had not said the last word about the centralization of authority. Dogma would certainly be developed in the future as it had been in the past. The Church did not regard its dogmas as the adequate expression of absolute truth, but as the least inadequate expression that had so far been possible.

As regards the Church's worship, Loisy argued that, if some Christian rites had had a non-Christian source and had been given a Christian interpretation, they were not for that reason alone to be condemned. 'The institutions, the external and traditional forms, which are indispensable to the existence and preservation of a religion, are necessarily adapted, in one way or another, to the milieu in which they take their shape' (p. 229). The Gentiles were not bound to all the customs of Judaism, and they were entitled to preserve their own usages, provided they were given a Christian sense.

And Loisy concluded his defence of the Christian religion with this at once weighty and modest passage:

It is true that, in consequence of the political, intellectual and economic evolution of the contemporary world, in consequence of what one may call the modern spirit, there is a great religious crisis more or less everywhere, and it affects Churches, orthodoxies and forms of worship. The best way of meeting it does not seem to be to suppress all ecclesiastical organization, all the orthodoxies and all traditional forms of worship: to do that would be to cast Christianity outside of life and of humanity. A better course is to make the best of what is in view of what ought to be, to repudiate none of the heritage which the Christian centuries have transmitted to ours, to recognize the necessity and the utility of the immense development that has taken place in the Church, to reap its fruits and to continue it, because the adaptation of the gospel to the changing condition of humanity is requisite today as always and more than ever.

It has not been part of the object of the present book to say what difficulties—perhaps more apparent than real—this task may encounter in the Catholic Church, nor what incomparable resources are available for this great work, nor how it may be possible, at the present time, to imagine an accord of dogma and science, of reason and faith, and of the Church and society. If I have succeeded in showing that Christianity has lived in the Church and by the Church and that it is futile to want to save it by looking for its quintessence, this little volume will have done enough (pp. 274f.).

It had in fact done enough. Loisy's qualified hope that the difficulties to be encountered in the Catholic Church might be more apparent than real was put to the test by the publication of *L'Évangile et l'Église* itself. While some eminent Catholics welcomed the book, it at once gave rise to a protracted series of controversies.[1] What was more serious, *L'Évangile et l'Église* was promptly censured by the Cardinal Archbishop of Paris, whose outlook was rigidly conservative. However, only seven French bishops followed suit and Rome was silent, so that the issue still seemed to be open.

It was Loisy's publication of a sequel a year later, together with his commentary on the Fourth Gospel, that brought matters to a head and led to Rome's demand for an abject retractation. It was now clear to Loisy that Rome would not allow him to continue his critical work on the Bible, and this killed his confidence in the Church. He was from this time prepared for the final rupture which took place in 1908. In the year after that, he was elected to the professorship at the Collège de France which had been vacated by the death of Jean Réville.

[1] Surveyed by Dr Emile Poulat in his interesting book, *Histoire, Dogme et Critique dans la Crise Moderniste* (1962).

The Church had rejected his defence of the Christian religion, and in his view the Church's judgment must be accepted as final. I find that English Protestants do not easily understand Loisy's abandonment of his Christian profession. The English tend to suppose that anyone who wishes to do so is entitled to call himself a Christian without regard to membership of a church. This subjective and individualistic attitude had never seemed reasonable to Loisy. He took it for granted that to be a Christian meant to be a member of a church, and it was for the Church to say who were and who were not its members. An individual professing to be a Christian without being a member of a church was a contradiction in terms.

Consequently, when the Roman Church excommunicated him, he accepted its verdict. He ceased to be a Catholic, and *a fortiori* a Catholic Modernist. His subsequent career is not our present concern, nor is the question, which has been much disputed, whether he had in effect ceased to be a Christian believer when he wrote *L'Évangile et l'Église*. I visited M. Loisy more than once in the 1930s, and I can only say that for my part I do not doubt the sincerity of his faith and of his allegiance to the Church up to the time when the Church demanded a retractation of his modernist convictions.

TYRRELL AT THE CROSS ROADS

Although Loisy himself ceased to hold the Catholic Modernist position which he had adumbrated and done more than anyone else to advertise, there were other Catholics who continued to hold it. Most notably was this the case with Father George Tyrrell. Tyrrell, unlike Loisy, continued to be a Catholic Modernist after his excommunication, and in fact when he died in 1909 he had just completed his last book, *Christianity at the Cross Roads*, of which a new edition was published in 1963.

Tyrrell was an Irishman, but he was not a cradle Catholic like Loisy. He had been converted to Roman Catholicism

from high anglicanism as a young man, and had become a
Jesuit and also a well-qualified scholastic theologian. It was
von Hügel who opened his mind to the limitations of
scholastic orthodoxy and in particular introduced him to the
critical study of Christian origins—in which field he was
never an expert like Loisy. Tyrrell was probably at his best
as a writer on the spiritual life—that was his proper *métier*.
But he had a restless, searching mind, and could never be
content till he had plumbed the profound questions which
new knowledge and ways of thinking were raising for
Catholicism. He threw himself into the modernist movement with ardour and prophetic fervour. He was bolder in
speculation than Loisy and also more recklessly outspoken.
His convictions as a Catholic Modernist were not stifled but
intensified by the Vatican's rejection of them.

His book, *Christianity at the Cross Roads*, was his last
and most ambitious expression of them. While confessedly
indebted to *L'Évangile et l'Église*, it carries that book's defence of Catholicism to lengths which Loisy never envisaged.
Tyrrell too had an exquisitely limpid style of writing, though
he did not live to revise his last book, and the writing is
somewhat uneven. It contains some of his memorable
epigrams such as 'If Rome dies, other churches may order
their coffins' (p. 29).

Shortly before writing his book, Tyrrell had read
Schweitzer's *Von Reimarus zu Wrede*,[1] and its thorough-
going eschatological interpretation of the gospel of Jesus,
which he had accepted with characteristic readiness, had
brought home to him more forcibly than ever the objections
to Liberal Protestantism, and at the same time the problem
of relating the eschatological or apocalyptic picture of Christ
with Catholicism.

His polemic against the Liberal Protestants was more
passionate than Loisy's and also more ironical.

[1] The English translation, *The Quest of the Historical Jesus*, had not yet
appeared.

They wanted to bring Jesus into the nineteenth century as the Incarnation of its ideal of Divine Righteousness, i.e. of all the highest principles and aspirations that ensure the healthy progress of civilization. . . . With eyes thus preoccupied they could only find the German in the Jew; a moralist in a visionary; a professor in a prophet; the nineteenth century in the first; the natural in the supernatural (p. 47).

According to Liberal Protestantism, he says:

No sooner was the Light of the World kindled than it was put under a bushel. The Pearl of Great Price fell into the dust-heap of Catholicism, not without the wise permission of Providence, desirous to preserve it till the day when Germany should rediscover it and separate it from its useful but deplorable accretions (*ibid.*).

It was in this connexion that Tyrrell coined his well-known aphorism:

The Christ that Harnack sees, looking back through nineteen centuries of Catholic darkness, is only the reflection of a Liberal Protestant face, seen at the bottom of a deep well (p. 49).

But the heart of Tyrrell's book is an attempt to show that the 'idea' (a word which he uses in Newman's sense) of the Christ of eschatology whose 'work on earth was to prepare and hasten the Kingdom—to close the last chapter of human history'—the mysterious, transcendental Christ who was 'incognito' during his ministry (p. 51)—was embodied and developed in Catholicism, and that there was no chasm between the Gospel and the Church.

The apocalyptic Kingdom of heaven was a valid symbol of the true End of man's existence. It stands for 'a bliss into which all may enter and not merely a favoured and final generation in a remote future' (p. 93). It should be remarked that, writing in 1909, Tyrrell welcomes apocalypticism because it challenges contemporary assumptions about progress which were so congenial to Liberal Protestants. He speaks of

> Liberal Protestantism, with its bland faith and hope in the present order, its refusal to face the incurable tragedy of human life—a tragedy that grows deeper as man rises from the hand-to-mouth simplicity of mere animal existence, extends his knowledge and control of experience and wakes ever more fully to the sense of his insatiable exigencies (p. 95).

Again he writes:

> At present the world that is heard and seen in public, elated with the success of science and the triumphs of invention, confident that what has done so much will do everything, is blind to the appalling residue of human misery and to the insoluble problems that are coming up slowly like storm-clouds on the horizon (p. 111).

Whereas, he says, for Christ

> the world was as good as finished and its final state was one of universal failure and illusion, not one of a proximate perfection that was all but Paradise. Well for the poor, the afflicted, the oppressed, who had lost all hope in it! . . . It was the poor who were ready for the Gospel of another life—not for the Gospel of social development (p. 116).

> To thrust immortality into the background, as a dim possibility that has not much to do with our Christianity; to make the reign of morality on earth . . . the whole meaning of the Kingdom of God and of eternal life, is to abandon, not religion, but the religion of Christ . . . it is . . . to make what is conditional principal; what is principal, subsidiary. . . . The emphasis of Christianity is on the whole life of the Spirit, viewed as a divine and eternal life, to be fully revealed only in its proper transcendental environment (p. 110).

Catholicism, Tyrrell argues, is true to the Gospel of Christ just because it has preserved the transcendental otherworldly perspective that was revealed in the eschatological framework of the original gospel. In other words, Tyrrell correlates Catholicism with the original gospel much more definitely and confidently than Loisy had done.

There is a shorter second part of *Christianity at the Cross Roads*, in which Tyrrell, in the light of the comparative study of religions and the psychology of religion, asks what prospect there is of the development of a universal religion, and he suggests that Catholicism—the Catholicism that is still alive within that Church which is at present being exploited by the Roman bureaucracy—that a transformed Catholicism has more promise of becoming a universal religion than any other since it

> is more nearly a microcosm of the world of religions than any other known form; where we find nearly every form of religious expression, from the lowest to the highest, pressed together and straining towards unification and coherence; where the ideal of universal and perpetual validity has ever been an explicit aim; where, moreover, this ideal is clothed in a form that cannot possibly endure the test of history and science and must undergo some transformation (p. 167).

Tyrrell's defence of the Christian religion is therefore more radical than Loisy's and, we may add, the outcome of a more fervent faith. Loisy's comment in his *Mémoires* (iii. 139) on *Christianity at the Cross Roads* is to the point:

> Between [Tyrrell's] modernism and that of *L'Évangile et L'Église* there is the distance which separates a very ardent mysticism from the simple examination of a given belief, of a given situation. Of *L'Évangile et l'Église* it has been said that it was quite Catholic, but hardly Christian in the Protestant sense of the word. Tyrrell's book, on the other hand, is thoroughly Christian, but hardly Catholic.

I hope from what I have said it will be seen that the common allegation that Catholic Modernists like Loisy and Tyrrell drove a wedge between the Jesus of history and the Christ of faith and were not really interested in the Jesus of history is unwarranted.[1] It was because they were so interested in the Jesus of history that they became modernists.

LE ROY ON DOGMA

Finally, I want to bring into the picture another example of Catholic Modernism of a more philosophical type. M. Édouard Le Roy was, as I have said, a layman. He was considerably influenced by the philosophy of Bergson, whose deputy he was for some years, and to whose chair of philosophy at the Collège de France he succeeded in 1921. But Le Roy was an original thinker, well versed in theology as in philosophy. He tells us that he had worked out his views about the nature of dogma before ever he read any of M. Loisy's books. There were affinities between his thought and that of the other French philosophical Modernists—Blondel and Laberthonnière—but they each worked independently and did not form a school.

Le Roy entered the fray in April 1905 with an article entitled *Qu'est-ce qu'un dogme?* ('What is a dogma?') which started an extensive controversy. He republished the article together with some substantial replies to his critics in the book *Dogme et Critique* (1907). It was this book that was put on the index. Le Roy made a formal submission and so did not incur excommunication. On the other hand, he did not abandon his ideas.

In the article 'What is a dogma?' he said that as a philosopher he was simply putting a question to the theologians and not propounding an answer, but he did not really conceal the fact that he had an answer to propound. He approached the subject as a layman whose duty it was to defend the Christian religion. 'Every layman in our days', he

---

[1] E.g. an editorial in the *Church Quarterly Review*, Oct.-Dec. 1962, p 398, speaks of 'the position of the Roman Catholic Modernists with their insistence on the Christ of faith and indifference to the Jesus of history'.

said, 'is called to do his duty as an apostle in the unbelieving world in which he lives' (p. 1).[1] He must therefore know what is the right way to defend the faith. It was obvious that the traditional way of putting things no longer made any impact on people whose intelligence had been trained in the disciplines of science and contemporary philosophy. The trouble was that the old style apologetic assumed that the basic questions had already been answered and proceeded at once to deal with secondary questions. It was necessary to begin all over again.

In the case of dogma, for example, the question: what is a dogma? should be faced before this or that particular dogma was commended. 'Men of today', he said, 'are within their rights in refusing to be bound by the standpoint of the 13th century' (p. 4). 'The very idea of dogma is now repugnant, and a source of scandal' (p. 6). Why? Le Roy gives four main reasons for the objections to dogma as it was commonly presented.

(1) A dogma appeared to be a proposition that was said to be intrinsically true, neither proved nor provable. But nowadays men rightly want to be shown that there are reasonable grounds for belief.

(2) If reasons for accepting dogmatic propositions are forthcoming, they take the form of an appeal to a transcendent authority that is supposed, as it were, to introduce the truth into us from outside. A dogma thus seems to be an external fetter, a limit set to thought, a sort of intellectual tyranny, denying man's need to be autonomous and sincere.

(3) Allowing for the sake of argument that dogmas could be simply taught by a doctrinal authority, they would in that case have to be intelligible and unambiguous. But the trouble with traditional Christian dogmas was that they were expressed in philosophical terminology—whether neo-

---

[1] References are to the 5th edition of *Dogme et Critique*.

platonic or aristotelian—which was no longer acceptable, or in metaphorical or anthropomorphic language which was merely confusing. 'In short,' says Le Roy, 'the first difficulty which numbers of people today find when confronted with dogmas is that they do not convey to them any intelligible meaning. These statements say nothing to them, or rather seem to them to be indissolubly bound up with a state of mind which is no longer theirs. . . . Many believers are implicitly of the same opinion and so prefer to abstain from reflecting on their faith' (p. 11).

(4) There is the grave objection that dogmas do not cohere with the rest of knowledge. Dogmas too are supposed to be immutable while thought is always progressive. Dogmas do not throw any light on scientific or philosophical problems. They do not connect.

These objections are decisive and unanswerable, Le Roy says, if the intellectualist conception of dogma is correct, i.e. if a dogma is taken to be a theoretical statement, a matter of pure knowledge. And that is how dogma is commonly regarded. God, in the act of revelation, is looked upon as a very wise professor whose word must be accepted when he imparts to his auditory conclusions of which it is incapable of understanding the proof.

For instance, if the dogma 'God is personal' is viewed in this way, as a statement of theoretical truth, then we are landed with the impossible problem of ascribing to the divine being 'personality' which is a concept derived from human psychology: we are landed in either anthropomorphism or agnosticism.

Likewise with the dogma of the resurrection of Jesus; if this is regarded as a piece of intellectual knowledge we are face to face with insurmountable difficulties about the relation between the kind of life that is ascribed to Jesus before and after his death.

Or again, with the dogma of the real presence in the

eucharist, 'presence' here cannot mean what it means in ordinary human thought. Intellectually, it is impossible to say precisely what it means.

The intellectualist conception of dogma, which supposes its primary function to be the communication of theoretical knowledge, breaks down everywhere.

Le Roy goes on to propose an alternative way of regarding dogmas. Intellectually, they have only a negative function. They do not convey positive knowledge, but are a warning against false notions. This is the *via negativa* that has been recognized in traditional theology but has been largely forgotten. 'From a strictly intellectual point of view, dogmas have only a negative or prohibitive sense. If they formulated absolute truth in adequate terms (supposing such a fiction had any sense) they would be unintelligible to us' (p. 23). On the other hand, if their truth were only imperfect, relative and changing, it would not be right to impose them.

This brings Le Roy to his main point, which is that dogmas have above all a *practical* sense. A dogma is primarily a rule of practical conduct and as such can be accepted by all believers in the same way, which could never be the case with theoretical statements. Religion is less an intellectual adherence to a system of speculative propositions than a lived participation in mysterious realities, and dogmas are guides to this participation.

So 'God is personal' means 'conduct yourselves in your relations with God as in your relations with a human person'. 'Jesus is risen' means 'regard him as you would have done before his death, as you would a contemporary'. The 'real presence' means that your attitude to the consecrated host should be what it would be if you saw Jesus face to face.

'Christianity in fact', concludes Le Roy, '—this cannot be too often repeated—is by no means a system of speculative philosophy, but a source and a rule of life, a discipline of moral and religious action' (p. 26).

Thus summarized, Le Roy's defence of Christian or

Catholic dogma may appear crude, but in the whole volume *Dogme et Critique* he works it out with great skill and he certainly has an answer to all the obvious criticisms. He is not afraid of the word 'pragmatism', though he says he does not use the word in the sense of William James. And indeed in the end Le Roy's position is nothing like so anti-intellectualist as may appear at first sight.

Whatever may be thought of it, I personally commend the sentiment with which Le Roy ends his book, and I would apply it to all the 'theological fashions' which I am considering in these lectures—fashions which their advocates incline to treat as opposed to one another:

> To my opponents whom I wish to regard as my friends, I confidently address . . . this appeal before God: let us help one another to grow in the truth and let us strive for unity rather than to triumph over one another. We profess the same faith, we share in the same life, we are committed to the same obedience, we have communion in the same prayer, we have at heart the same desire and the same love (p. 344).

3

English Liberal Catholicism

THE MODERNIST movement in the Roman Church was followed with interest and sympathy by a good many Anglo-Catholics—at least in its early stages. For instance, in 1904 T. A. Lacey, one of the most learned of them, published a lecture entitled *Harnack and Loisy*, in which he said :

> For Harnack, Jesus of Nazareth is an isolated personage, promulgating one great thought which is to abide for ever unchanged. For Loisy, Jesus of Nazareth is an historical personage, who gathers up the Jewish ideas of the Messianic Kingdom and gives them a new direction, leaving them to be fruitful of immense developments. Which is the true conception? (p. 11).

With few qualifications, Lacey said that he was sure Loisy was right. Charles Gore had said the same in 1901, though he would not have said so later.[1] Viscount Halifax, most eminent of Anglo-Catholic laymen, contributed an introductory letter to Lacey's lecture in which he expressed the hope that the Holy Office would not commit the blunder of condemning Loisy. Lacey was at this time on the staff of the *Church Times*, the weekly organ of Anglo-Catholicism, which in the following years showed a lively interest in what the Roman Modernists were attempting to do. It is, however, to some other English Liberal Catholics that I want to direct your attention in this lecture.

[1] See letter of 13 May 1901 from Gore to von Hügel in St Andrews University Library.

The term 'Liberal Catholic' has been applied to various groups and individuals in both the Roman and Anglican Churches. Lamennais and those associated with him in the *Avenir* were known as Liberal Catholics: in that case 'Liberal' had primarily a political connotation. Döllinger and Acton were Liberal Catholics in an intellectual sense. But the ambiguity of the expression is seen in the fact that Newman can be described as a Liberal Catholic, i.e. *vis-à-vis* ultramontanism, although he was a life-long opponent of what he called 'liberalism', i.e. the Liberalism which the Tractarians had attacked. Again, F. D. Maurice has been called a Liberal Catholic in contrast to the Tractarians. At the end of the century Wilfrid Ward, Newman's biographer, was known as a Liberal Catholic, which meant that his position, while not ultramontane or intransigent like that of his father, was more orthodox and moderate than that of the Catholic Modernists.

In the Church of England the first group to welcome the name for themselves were the authors of *Lux Mundi*, the volume of essays, published in 1889, which was a deliberate attempt to restate the theology of the Tractarians in the light of new scientific knowledge and the critical study of the Bible. Charles Gore, their chief, gloried in the title 'Liberal Catholic'.[1] From that time onwards there were within the Anglo-Catholic movement both liberal and conservative wings, and within the liberal wing there were considerable varieties and advances. It is about some of them that I am going to speak in this lecture.

I am not going to deal with Gore himself, for more than one reason. On the one hand, Gore's Liberal Catholicism had finally crystallized before the end of the 19th century, i.e. before my period. He continued to maintain his position till his death in 1932, but he did not make any advance upon it, and in fact found himself at odds with a new generation of English Liberal Catholics. And, on the

[1] See my *Essays in Liberality* (1957), chapter vii.

other hand, an excellent book on Gore's Liberal Catholicism was published a few years ago—*Gore: a Study in Liberal Catholic Thought* by James Carpenter (1960). He also figures largely in the Archbishop of Canterbury's book *From Gore to Temple* (1960).

FIGGIS ON CIVILIZATION'S CONFUSION

I am going to consider some Liberal Catholics whose thought matured after 1900 and who worked out new or distinctive ways of defending the Christian religion. I take first John Neville Figgis (1886-1919), who in some respects stood nearer to Gore than the others—and not only because he joined the Community of the Resurrection of which Gore was the founder.

Figgis was the son of a distinguished nonconformist minister of the Countess of Huntingdon's Connexion, and the evangelical upbringing he received left a permanent impress on his outlook. He had a brilliant career at Cambridge and became a history don. As an historian, he was a follower of Maitland, Mandell Creighton and Acton. When he was a young man he went through a period of agnosticism, before he settled for ordination in the Church of England. There was indeed a strong strain of *intellectual* scepticism in his make-up. Like Édouard Le Roy, Figgis was much attracted by the anti-intellectualist philosophy of Henri Bergson. So in one of his books we find him writing, characteristically :

Bergson's theory of the inward nature of all living knowledge is also that of the world at large, outside the philosophic paddock. No one could learn by theory how to play football or even what it was like. Speculation can give no even approximate account of the experience of love or hate, or even the sensation as felt of colour or music. Life is inexhaustibly concrete and everlastingly strange; however much scientific external method may tell us about its outward aspects; that can never even approximate to a representtion of what it means inwardly to do or refuse an act of courage, to grieve over sins, or to be transfigured by love.[1]

Figgis also quoted with approval the remark: 'In future we may be pro-Bergsonians or anti-Bergsonians, but we shall all be post-Bergsonians.'[2] (Incidentally, I remember a friend of mine in the army during the first World War making just that remark to me: this was before I had ever read a word of Bergson myself.)

Figgis was also increasingly attracted to Anglo-Catholicism as it seemed to him a richer embodiment of the Christian faith than what he had been accustomed to: its sacramentalism, its emphasis on the communion of saints, its combination of world-affirmation with world-renunciation, particularly appealed to him. And it was under this impulse that he eventually resigned the fat college living in Dorsetshire, to which he had been appointed, in order to become a Mirfield monk. This was to the surprise, if not the consternation, of his friends: for Figgis was extremely convivial, a great mixer and conversationalist, a *bon viveur*, not at all a natural ascetic or self-disciplinarian. But that of course made his action all the more significant. He now began to exert an extensive influence as a prophetic preacher, while at the same time he continued with his historical work.

I take one of his books, *Civilisation at the Cross Roads*, as representative, partly because it connects with George Tyrrell's *Christianity at the Cross Roads*. *Civilisation at the Cross Roads* consisted of the William Belden Noble lectures which Figgis delivered at Harvard in 1911. In the preface he said that his title

might seem to imply that I desire to controvert the main thesis of the late Father Tyrrell's famous work. This, however, is not the case. Too greatly am I in debt to all the writings of that arresting author and especially to his posthumous work to have any such thought (p. ix).

[1] See M. G. Tucker, *John Neville Figgis* (1950), p. 33.
[2] *Civilisation at the Cross Roads* (1912), p. 40.

All the same, he did have something of such a thought, and his title has an incisive point in relation to Tyrrell's.[1]

Would it not be true to say that all the 'defenders of the Christian religion' whom I have so far considered in these lectures (with the exception of Tyrrell?)—the Liberal Protestants and the Catholic Modernists—had taken it for granted that the modern world was a good thing which had come to stay and steadily to progress? Their problem had been how to adapt or reinterpret the Christian religion so that it could be in harmony with new scientific and historical knowledge and with the new philosophical climate. In a word, the Christian religion needed to be so transformed or adjusted that it could cohabit with modern civilization.

The *title* of Tyrrell's book had certainly given the impression that Christianity had to decide whether or not to move in that direction. Figgis took this to be Tyrrell's contention. 'The assumption', he writes, 'at the basis of George Tyrrell's *Christianity at the Cross Roads* seems to be that wherever Christianity conflicts with our modern mental scheme, it must be trimmed to make the two square' (p. 171). I do not think that is fair to Tyrrell himself, but it was at least a plausible criticism of the Liberal Protestants and the Catholic Modernists as a whole.

Now Figgis—although he was no reactionary or theological obscurantist—had a very different theme. It was civilization, rather than the Gospel or the Church, that was under judgment and in peril of collapse—though he granted, indeed stressed, the greatly diminished influence of Christianity. The best means of defence is said to be attack, and Figgis's defence of the Christian religion took the form of an attack on a civilization that had abandoned Christianity and could not be expected to recover without a return to the

[1] On 24 October 1909 G. C. Rawlinson wrote to von Hügel: 'Dr Figgis is by no means friendly to modernism of any kind.' (St Andrews University Library.)

faith—the faith of the Bible and of the evangelical and Catholic traditions.

So, for example, he writes:

> If the world is to be brought back to Christ, it will not be by accepting its shibboleths and seeing God's revelation through eyes purblind with avarice or satisfied with the things of this world, but rather by dwelling on the strange new life He promises and re-awakening that sense of sin which has become unfashionable (p. 26).

Figgis supports his thesis with a discriminating examination of the manifestations of contemporary culture in philosophy, literature, art and politics.

> We live in an age of unparalleled anarchy both moral and intellectual. The confusion of tongues is worse than in any Babel of old (p. 34).

Modern intellectuals agree in nothing but in their rejection of, or indifference to, the Christian faith.

> What is there positive to set in its place? This question remains without reply. Scientific materialism is not held as a creed except by a few, is commonly declared not to be one, although its presuppositions rule men's minds to a larger extent than they know. Beyond that all is chaos. Positivists, agnostics, idealists, pessimists, optimists, sceptics, theists, atheists jostle one another and nobody knows what his next-door neighbour thinks. And that even among reflecting and cultivated men, who are above the mere vulgarities of money-making (p. 36).

Twenty years before there had been a general acceptance of some form of idealist philosophy, but that had now gone the way of all flesh. Perhaps it would be true now to say that 'there is general agreement to adopt a purely agnostic standpoint', and Figgis comments:

If we include the general level of educated and half-educated people, this would be nearer the truth. As a purely philosophic doctrine agnosticism is, of course, by no means incompatible with theistic or even Christian belief, and may make a very good basis for it (p. 43).

He cites A. J. Balfour as an example. But this was not what agnosticism meant to the generality. In practice it meant an acceptance of naturalism, and that was due to the success of physical science and its achievements which had issued from a method of inquiry that postulated the uniformity of nature. The modern prejudice against Christian faith, he writes,

has been created by the predominance of a single method, triumphant in its own sphere, and the attempt to carry it into regions where it is powerless (p. 61).

But in reality 'we have to do with a universe in which being exists on different levels. There is the mechanical level of the physicists, or inorganic Nature; there is the sentient life of the animal world; and the character-making, active life of man; in the latter we discern alike in ourselves and others many different levels—the emotional, the intellectual, the spiritual. All are interpenetrating and none (probably not even the mechanism of Nature) exist in active isolation' (p. 265).

Scientific naturalism was qualified to deal with the mechanism of nature, but it was powerless to account for personal existence, for human freedom, and the overarching mysteries into which everything runs out at last. So he drives home his challenge:

There is an irreconcilable conflict, not indeed between science and religion, but between scientific fatalism and the postulates of the Christian Faith (p. 147).

Either the whole world, seen no less than unseen, is conceived as personal, spiritual, alive, ever fresh . . . or else it is seen

as mechanical, impersonal, dead, with human history un-
rolling itself, like a cinematograph. The one is the world of
Catholic Christianity, the other that of Pagan philosophy or
scientific fatalism and its more spiritual or at least decorative
variety—Pantheism (p. 72).

Then he points out that modern civilization for all its
boasted triumphs acquiesces in appalling social injustice.
And again psychological disease was on the increase. ' "There
is death in the pot" of modern civilisation,' he exclaims, 'and
it is not like to heal itself' (p. 91).

It was redemption that civilization needed. 'The crying
need of the time is for something to shake men out of their
complacency. In the literal sense we need seers—men who
can see things as they are and burn into men the facts of life
in this twentieth century' (p. 116).

It is a new soul that the world needs, not a scheme of reforms.
The only source of such new life is faith of one kind or
another. From many observers comes the cry for life, for
deliverance, for some uplifting power. The cry, though little
regarded as yet in the seats of the mighty, will ere long be
triumphant, unless the world is to go the way of other
decadent civilisations and pass through self-indulgence to
ruin (pp. 104f.).

It was not the reduced Christianity of Liberal Protestantism that was needed, and anyhow that was being
shaken to pieces by apocalypticism.

Dr Schweitzer . . . has declared that if Jesus Christ came into
our modern world, He would come as a stranger; that our
characteristic categories hold no place for Him; that the funda-
mentally other-worldly claim, the apocalyptic vision of Jesus
is opposed to the presuppositions of the ordinary educated
man, formed as they are under the influence of naturalism.
I believe that Dr Schweitzer is right (p. 147).

But Figgis draws a different conclusion from Schweitzer's:

If . . . you accept the lordship of Jesus as a mysterious being, with something in Him more than human, you will be carried, however reluctantly, to the Christ of the Creeds and the New Testament and the whole supernatural faith in a Church dispensing gifts of God's grace and guided by a power not of this world (pp. 155f.).

What was at stake, Figgis maintained, was the freedom of man which was bound up with the freedom of God. He granted that neither admitted of proof, at any rate according to the criteria of naturalism. He granted that there were historical perplexities, and greater difficulties still. 'I do not deny', he said,

the extreme difficulty of the fundamental faith of the Christian in Love, as Lord of all things. The doctrine of the Fatherhood of God, to which some would fain reduce Christianity, in the hope of making it easy and universal, is to me the profoundest of all stumbling blocks (pp. 214f.).

But whatever the difficulties of belief he found that every alternative was even worse. Figgis is then an example of what has been called 'the sceptical approach to religious belief',[1] but there was nothing hesitant in the delivery of his message.

I said that he was a prophetic preacher. His style and his themes had much in common with those of his contemporary, P. T. Forsyth, who was saying as a Free Churchman what Figgis was saying as an Anglican. There was an affinity between them both and Mr G. K. Chesterton. All three were highly rhetorical and addicted to startling epigrams. They supplied a wholesome challenge and corrective to prevalent trends in Christian apologetic, but they tended to depreciate the need for restating the grounds for Christian belief in as cool and lucid and precise a manner as was possible. What the Liberal Protestants and the Catho-

[1] See Paul Elmer More's book *The Sceptical Approach to Religion* (1934).

lic Modernists had sought to do still needed to be done, and there were other English Liberal Catholics who addressed themselves to this task.

QUICK AND CHRISTOLOGY

I turn now to Oliver Chase Quick (1885-1944), who was finally Regius Professor of Divinity at Oxford. He was, as William Temple said, 'a theologian of penetrating insight and wide comprehension'[1]—an independent mind, not a member of any close group or school. I do not remember anyone who struck me as so formidably acute in argument.

In one of his books, *Liberalism, Modernism and Tradition*, the Bishop Paddock Lectures given in New York in 1922, he set himself to assess the christology of Liberal Protestantism, Catholic Modernism and traditional orthodoxy, and in the light of his assessment to suggest a new christology or a new orthodoxy that would do justice to the truth which he recognized in all three. Quick was a philosophical and dogmatic theologian, not an historian, and he handled his subject schematically.

He started by saying that it was a characteristic of modern theology to distinguish between facts and beliefs, though in a sense beliefs, whether true or false, are also facts. Anyhow, unlike traditional orthodoxy, the critical historian distinguishes between the actual events which were the origin of Christianity and the progressive interpretation or valuation of those events which determined the subsequent development of the Christian Church. The question inevitably arose whether the original facts justified the subsequent interpretation.

In this situation two courses were open : one of which was adopted by the Liberal Protestants, following Ritschl, and the other by Catholic Modernists like Loisy and Tyrrell.

[1] Prefatory memoir to Quick's book, *The Gospel of a New World* (1944), p. xiv.

C

On the one hand, it was possible to exalt the value and importance of the original facts . . ., to maintain that in them is the essence of Christianity, and to disparage and discount subsequent doctrines, which they do not seem to justify. . . .

On the other hand, it was possible to attach primary value and importance to the ideas underlying the developments of doctrine . . . and to find the essential truth of Christianity in their continuous growth and expansion in the minds of men (p. 3).

The watchword of Liberal Protestantism, which had adopted the former course, had been 'Back to the historical Jesus'. If divinity was ascribed to him, it was on the ground that in a unique way he was a living example and embodiment of his own teaching about the Fatherhood of God. Are we not justified, the Liberal Protestant asked, in calling uniquely divine a man who so uniquely and finally expressed and interpreted God to us? Quick acknowledged the genuine pastoral fervour of theologians like Harnack. They had succeeded in presenting Christianity in a way that attracted the plain man who was repelled by what seemed to him metaphysical and mystical subtleties. The Liberal Protestants had done a good service in insisting that the doctrine of Christ's Person is not a speculative dogma to be accepted on authority but an attempt to express the experience of believers who had been brought into communion with God through Jesus Christ. But their mistake or their shortcoming had been to isolate the Jesus of the synoptic gospels, instead of emphasizing the continuity of his life and influence in the Risen Christ of the Church.

The Catholic Modernists, on the other hand, had adopted the second course. They had taken a hint, and more than a hint, from Newman, who in his *Essay on Development* had written :

It is sometimes said that the stream is clearest near the spring. Whatever use may fairly be made of this image, it does not apply to the history of a philosophy or a belief which, on the contrary, is more equable, and purer, and stronger when its bed has become deep, and broad, and full. . . . Its beginnings are no measure of its capabilities, nor of its scope. At first no one knows what it is, or what it is worth. . . . It tries, as it were, its limbs and proves the ground under it, and feels its way. . . . In a higher world it is otherwise, but here below to live is to change, and to be perfect is to have changed often (pp. 27f.).

The Catholic Modernists applied this notion in a way Newman never contemplated. In contrast to the Liberal Protestants they regarded idea rather than fact as the basis of Christianity; they regarded development rather than origin as the essence of Christianity; and they opposed the community to the individual as the organ of Christianity. For them

> Jesus was . . . a man possessed by a tremendous idea, too great, too eternal, to be given any adequate expression in the categories of thought and language belonging to any one place or time. Like all other men, he had to incarnate the idea in the flesh of His own individuality, and to give it expression in the only language and thought which He Himself and His contemporaries . . . could understand (i.e. the eschatological Kingdom and the Messiahship). . . . The spirit, the idea, the eternal truth, live and exist for us only through changing expression in developing forms, and therein lies the justification for the Catholic Church of history, whose glory it is that she offers to men the same essential Gospel of Jesus not in spite of, but because of, the differences she has made in it. (pp. 34f.).

Quick granted that Catholic Modernism had got hold of something valid and important in its conception of the essence of Christianity as its wholeness and of the contribution to that wholeness which is made by historical development. His objection to it was that it justified too much: it had no criterion with which to judge what was a true and what was a false development. And anyhow it had been disowned by the Church which it had intended to vindicate.

But he has a more fundamental criticism of both the Liberal Protestants and the Catholic Modernists.

> Somehow (he says) the orthodox Christian feels that the Being Whom he calls God has been left out of the intellectual constructions of both parties, or at least is only brought back and retained inconsistently by an effort of faith or emotion which does not fit into either system as a whole (p. 53).

Quick then turns to consider traditional orthodoxy which, he says, was compounded of Jewish supernaturalism and of Platonic philosophy. They were uneasy bedfellows, but out of them the doctrine of the two natures of Christ in one Person had been wrought in an attempt to do justice to the facts of Christian experience. The doctrine arose from a belief in two worlds which, in different forms, had been axiomatic for both the Jews and the Greeks. This belief in two worlds had been discarded by modern thought which was essentially anthropocentric instead of theocentric. If it conceived of deity at all, it was in terms of immanence, not of transcendence.

Yet Quick did not suggest that a recovery of traditional orthodoxy in its traditional form was possible. In any case, it had conceived of the transcendence of God in terms of a crude interventionism, which would not do.

Quick then attempts to adumbrate a new christology— what he calls essential orthodoxy, which would do justice to the truth in 'liberalism, modernism and tradition'. He makes considerable concessions to the Catholic Modernists. 'The truest nature of a thing is its fullest development' (p. 141). It was the Christian experience of the new kind of *agape*, the new kind of fellowship with God and one another which the Risen Christ and his Spirit had created in the *koinonia* of the Church, that had led Christians to predicate deity of Jesus, and not what Jesus had said or done during his earthly life. 'It is', Quick says, 'an essentially impossible task to find the full Deity in Jesus Christ known *only* after the flesh, *i.e.* as a historic figure. . . . We must judge what was latent in the days of His flesh by what became patent only through the resurrection and ascension and the coming of the Holy Spirit' (pp. 141f.). But Quick holds that traditional orthodoxy had been right in predicating deity ontologically of the historic Jesus, which neither Catholic Modernism nor Liberal Protestantism appeared to do.

I confess I find Quick's attempt to be constructive highly speculative: he himself stressed its tentativeness, and I shall not try to summarize it. It was one of a number of essays made by English Liberal Catholics at that period to propound a christology that was at once traditional and in contemporary philosophical categories and consonant with the critical attitude to the New Testament. Other examples would be William Temple's *Christus Veritas* (1924) and L. S. Thornton's *The Incarnate Lord* (1928). A detached observer might say that they all illustrate the anglican partiality for a *via media*, or for having it both ways. A kinder verdict would be that they were temperamentally averse to following a single track. I do not think that any of them 'got across' in the way that Liberal Protestantism or Catholic Modernism did, or that they have carried any widespread conviction as defences of the Christian religion. Or perhaps I should say no more than that, so far as I am concerned, they did not get under my skin. Many other modern divines, it seems to me, have been, like Quick, much more effective in criticism than in construction.

SPENS ON BELIEF IN GOD

Figgis and Quick were influential but independent or singular Liberal Catholics. They were not members of a school as the *Lux Mundi* essayists may be said to have been. I turn next to a Liberal Catholic who was, and conceived himself to be, a member of a group or specific school of thought. I mean Mr, later Sir, Will Spens (1882-1962). I have in my possession a privately printed address which he gave in the U.S.A. in 1933 on 'The Present Position of the Catholic Movement in the Church of England'. In this address he claimed to be expressing the views of a group of Liberal Catholics who were mostly connected with Cambridge, where they had become associated in the years before the first World War. After the war the group enlarged its scope and its membership.

Writing in 1933, Spens names a number of its members including E. G. Selwyn (Dean of Winchester), Wilfred Knox (the N.T. scholar), A. E. J. Rawlinson (afterwards Bishop of Derby), and even myself though I was considerably junior to the rest. Rawlinson was an Oxford man, but an essay which he had contributed to the symposium entitled *Foundations* (1912) was regarded by this group as a signpost to the line of thought they were to develop. As regards myself, during the 1930s I was living with Wilfred Knox at Cambridge and collaborating with him, but so far as my experience went this so-called group of Cambridge Liberal Catholics was more loosely associated than, for example, the *Lux Mundi* essayists or than the much more recent group of theologians, of which I have also been a member, that produced the volume of essays entitled *Soundings* in 1962. In the 1930s we never had any formal meetings: but I grant that one had a sense of belonging and of being engaged in a common enterprise.

Spens himself was Tutor, and later Master, of Corpus Christi College, which was something of a centre for the group we are now considering, since E. G. Selwyn had connexions there, and among the Fellows of the College were Sir Edwyn Hoskyns, who was originally a member of the group but later took a line of his own (as I shall notice in my next lecture), and Dr R. H. Thouless, the psychologist. I may add for the record that while Corpus stood for liberalism in theology it also stood for conservatism in politics, but some of us who favoured the former were averse to the latter!

From 1920 this group had a monthly journal, *Theology*, of which Selwyn was the first editor,[1] and its members were mainly responsible for producing the volume *Essays Catholic and Critical* (1926), also edited by Selwyn, which was intended to mark a new stage in the development of the Liberal Catholicism that had made its début in *Lux Mundi*. But a book which is now less well known and which was always handicapped by its unattractive style was, I should say, more seminal for this group, namely *Belief and Practice* (1915) by Will Spens, and I propose now to say something about it. D. M. Baillie in his book *Faith in God and its Christian Consummation* (p. 129) pays tribute to the 'great subtlety' of Spens's argument.

Spens would not, I think, have objected to his book being described as a 'defence of the Christian religion', for he was certainly quite happy with the word 'religion'. He says that his purpose is 'to show that within certain limits we have in the Church's theology a system of thought which has a legitimate claim on men's acceptance' (p. v).[2] Spens was by training a scientist (he took a first in the Natural Sciences Tripos at Cambridge), and it would appear that he wanted to satisfy himself, as well as other people, that the authority claimed for theological beliefs was consonant with, or analogous to, the authority claimed for scientific beliefs.

If Spens was defending the Christian religion, it should be understood that he was defending it on various fronts. He was seeking to commend it to reasonable men who were disposed to regard it as unreasonable, and this involved distinguishing his own system from current ways of defending or commending the Christian religion, which he himself

[1] I observe that in July 1909 Selwyn had written to von Hügel to express his gratitude for what he owed to Tyrrell's writings. See von Hügel's papers in St Andrew's University Library.
[2] References are to the second edition of *Belief and Practice* (1917).

regarded as unreasonable or indefensible, in particular from Roman Catholicism and Liberal Protestantism.

On the first page of his book he says that religion should not be 'regarded as a hard-drawn system of thought' but as 'an imperfect but real insight, as an imperfect but growing knowledge of God, and as an imperfect but a substantial grasp of the possibilities of experience'. 'The fundamental issue', he says, 'is not whether certain doctrines are true or false, but as to our conception of doctrine. We have to consider whether theology should not regard, as its data, experience rather than propositions. . . . It is not minimized if we regard it as a revelation of, rather than about, God. . . . Such a view enables theology to take advantage of methods, of which the value is widely recognized' (pp. 7f.), i.e. scientific methods. If dogmas are treated 'as inferences from experience, we give to theology a far greater authority' than they could have if treated as oracular pronouncements guaranteed to be infallible by an external authority.

In view of the vital place that 'religious experience' has in Spens's thought, I should perhaps at this point say that when a reviewer of the first edition of his book had complained that 'those who appeal to religious experience do not make clear what they mean', Spens said—in a note appended to the second edition—that he thought the term had a meaning pretty generally accepted (this is to me both surprising and significant), but in order to meet his critic he went on to say that by religious experience he meant:

In the first place a very general experience of certain needs and capacities, and of the possibility of their satisfaction. Among the chief of these are a sense of incompleteness, its relief by religious practice, and its removal in the experience which religion describes as communion with God; the sense of duty and vocation; the sense of sin, repentance, and forgiveness; the capacity for worship; and the experience of moral and spiritual power resulting from religious practice. This last is sufficiently different from their other experiences as to lead its subjects to ascribe it, rightly or wrongly, to an external source. There may be added . . . the remarkable enhancement of such experiences in any great religious revival; the facilitation of very complete changes of character and feeling by religious beliefs in the phenomena of 'conversion'; and the curiously uniform experiences of the stricter mystics (p. 254).

It will be seen that by religious experience Spens did not mean mystical experience, nor the abnormalities studied by William James, but what he would call normal experience.

Spens says that he had been struck by a saying of Fr Tyrrell's 'that the dogmas of the Church must control theology in the same way in which the facts of science control science' (p. 22). For both of them, dogmas were inferences from experience. Spens conceived himself to be developing a suggestion which Tyrrell had not lived to work out himself, and on which in any case the Roman Church had put the lid. 'The theories of science', Spens said, 'have their significance in large measure, and have their primary authority, in the fact that they express, relate, and enable us to predict, available experience' (p. 23). Scientific theories (he supplies illustrations of them) are open to revision or more adequate formulation, but they are retained until others, of a more satisfactory character, can be found to cover the same experience. Further, a scientific theory is tested not only 'by its power to rationalize particular facts', but also 'by its power to produce a sound general outlook' (p. 26). Another point is that science rests upon certain fundamental assumptions, such as the uniformity of nature, which never have been completely verified, and are not capable of complete verification.

Spens then draws out the parallel with theology. He claims to show that there are

grounds for regarding the Catholic tradition of thought as having been evolved in close dependence on religious experience; as expressing, with marked and exceptional success, the possibilities of religious experience; as embodying a very wide range of such experience, and presenting by far the best available synthesis; as issuing in conceptions which have proved able to cover different fields of experience (p. 61).

What, on these grounds, he claims for theology is that it is not 'a complete metaphysic, but merely the expression of a growing insight into ultimate reality' (p. 62).

It follows that if theology is to have the kind of authority or title to belief that science has, theological thought must be genuinely free.

If theological thought is to possess any high degree of authority, not only must such thought be closely related to experience, but the consensus of opinion must be a free consensus. If you put, by means of ecclesiastical authority, a high premium on some particular opinion, then the evidential value of a consensus of thought in favour of that opinion is greatly weakened (p. 73).

In other words, an enforced unity is destructive of any rational authority for doctrine.

It is on one or other of these grounds that Liberal Protestantism and Roman Catholicism are found wanting. Liberal Protestantism bids us return to Jesus the Prophet, and disregards the argument from the whole corpus of Christian experience to 'those conceptions of an Incarnation and an Atonement, which hinge round the idea of a supernatural Christ' (p. 86). That is to say, its data are much too restricted.

Roman Catholicism, on the other hand, fails to meet the test, because although its doctrine is related to a very wide range of religious experience, it does not provide for a free consensus, and the doctrinal immobility, of which it boasts, tells in fact against it and weakens its rational authority.

As regards Catholic Modernism, while Spens considered that it—in particular, Fr Tyrrell—was moving in the right direction, he urged that it underestimated the force of the argument from Christian experience to the historical reality of the Incarnation, the Atonement and the supernatural Christ.

Nevertheless, he said that it was for time to show how far such a rejection of Modernism is well founded or whether rejection of it is merely the outcome of a natural conservatism. Spens argues strongly for the historicity of the Incarnation, but at the same time he allows that the Modernists were justified in holding that the value of Catholic doctrines would not vanish with the discovery that they were myth: they might still give real information about the nature and character of God. In saying this, Spens marked the extent of his difference—and of the difference of this Cambridge school—from another Liberal Catholic of the period who stood much more nearly in the Gore tradition, namely N. P. Williams, who said that if an *ostrakhon* were unearthed at Nazareth which showed conclusively that Joseph was the father of Jesus he would at once abandon the Christian faith and look round for some other theory of the universe.[1]

In the second part of his book, Spens applied his theory to the particular doctrines of Christology, the Eucharist, and the Church. In each case he follows Tyrrell in appealing to the evidential value of religious experience, but he arrives at more traditional orthodox conclusions, though not by any means at conventional ones. On re-reading *Belief and Practice* in preparation for this lecture, I have certainly been more impressed than ever by its subtlety, and also by the way in which it takes into account a wealth of considerations and possible objections, of which my very sketchy summary must have given a quite inadequate impression.

RAWLINSON ON DOGMA

In the same year as *Belief and Practice* was first published (1915), A. E. J. Rawlinson published a book entitled *Dogma, Fact and Experience* in one chapter of which he paid par-

[1] See W. Sanday and N. P. Williams, *Form and Content in the Christian Tradition* (1916), p. 90.

ticular attention to Édouard Le Roy's *Dogme et Critique* which Rawlinson describes, I think justly, as 'the ablest statement of the modernist view of dogma' (p. 32). He gives a summary of Le Roy's argument which, as you may recall, was to the effect that dogmas should not be regarded intellectualistically, as positive contributions to speculative knowledge. In so far as they have an intellectual function, it is a negative one: dogmas are a warning against certain errors or false paths. They rule out certain positions as inadequate. They do not guarantee the truth of any particular system of metaphysics. The positive function of dogmas, according to Le Roy, is not speculative but practical. They prescribe rules of practical conduct, as for instance that you should behave in your relations with God as you would in your relations with a human person. I need not recapitulate other examples.

Rawlinson recognizes that Le Roy's position is not simply the 'crude religious pragmatism' (pp. 35f.) that at first sight it may appear to be, since he makes two important provisos. First, that every dogmatic precept of the Church involves the *implicit* affirmation that Reality is of such a character as, in some real sense, to justify as right and reasonable the conduct which the dogma prescribes. And, secondly, that the acceptance of dogma as a rule of conduct must not exclude the duty of thought and the quest for an intellectual synthesis.

Rawlinson then says that, if Le Roy's teaching be considered purely 'as a philosophy of the significance and function of dogma in the life of a Churchman' (p. 37), he was personally disposed to accept the view. So far he would go along with the Catholic Modernist, but then he proceeds to say that Le Roy's teaching does not go to the root of the matter. I am not sure that Rawlinson interprets Le Roy quite correctly, but anyhow what is of interest to us now is Rawlinson's own reasons for regarding as inadequate what he takes to be Le Roy's view.

He says that it might satisfy a man who was already 'a

devout and practising Christian', who might continue to be so while being largely agnostic about ultimate questions. Rawlinson imagines such a man saying to himself:

> These practices of prayer and sacrament, and this dogmatic Catholic creed, have brought spiritual life and strength to me and to others in the past and can still do so in the future. I may be doubtful enough as to the alleged historical origins of my religion, and I may be unwilling to commit myself speculatively to Theism in any orthodox sense of the term; but I believe that there is a spiritual reality at the back of the world, and through these particular creeds and forms and symbols—imperfect, crude, and fumbling as I take them to be—I have found by experience that my finite spirit—so runs at least my dream—may hold communion with the Infinite (pp. 37f.).

But, continues Rawlinson, it is difficult to see how such a presentation or defence of the Christian religion could ever make much impression on anyone who was not already within the Christian fold. 'There is all the difference', he says, 'between religion advocated as a possible view of the universe and a helpful attitude to life, and religion proclaimed as the truth of God Himself and the very core of what life means' (pp. 38f.).

As a matter of history, Christianity has been proclaimed from the beginning as a Gospel, as good news about a living personal God, upon whom everything depends and who is ceaselessly operative and active, and in particular who comes to deliver man from his impotence to attain to communion with God by his own powers. Christianity is not a religion of man's search for God, but of God's search for man. And it was in the historic Person of Jesus Christ that the Life and Power of God were once for all manifested, and this action of God in Christ, his reconciling of the world unto himself, is for ever continued and perpetuated in the Church.

Such a Gospel 'cannot possibly be independent of all

imaginable conclusions, either of historical science or of philosophical speculation' (p. 47). In particular, says Rawlinson, 'the Gospel, divorced from its basis in history, must needs lose its essential power' (p. 49). He is prepared to allow considerable uncertainty about much of the detail recorded in the gospels, but in his view if the historical critic comes to conclusions which no longer enable him to say that God was in Christ reconciling the world unto himself, he is faced by a choice between abandoning the Gospel and modifying the presuppositions of his criticism.

It will be seen that Rawlinson, like Spens, appeals to religious experience, and he goes much of the way with the Catholic Modernists as he understands them. But he is more conclusive than Spens in affirming that Christianity is a Gospel that necessarily depends on historical credenda.

By and large, with differences of emphasis, this was the position of the English Liberal Catholics whom I have been considering in this lecture. It was a position that was as adverse to the Liberal Protestant defence of the Christian religion as Catholic Modernism had been. It was a position that acknowledged sympathy with, and indebtedness to, the Catholic Modernists or some of them, but that claimed to be a more adequate interpretation and defence of what was involved in the total experience of the Catholic Church.

But rude shocks were in store for the Liberal Catholics as well as for all other theological modernizers.

4

Neo-Orthodoxy

IN THE three previous lectures I was dealing with 'theological fashions' or ways of defending the Christian religion that were characteristic of what could be accounted distinct 'schools of thought', though none of them had anything like the organization of an ecclesiastical party. Also, they could by now be seen in historical perspective and be viewed with a becoming detachment. Neither of these things can be said of the subjects of my last two lectures. My titles—Neo-Orthodoxy and Christian Radicalism—are intended, both of them, to cover a variety of trends or tendencies of thought which, so far as I can see, have much less coherence or specifiable common character, though of course this may be only because I cannot yet see them in historical perspective. The trends or tendencies I have in mind are still very much with us and maybe *in* us. Anyhow, it is less easy to survey them with that kind of objectivity after which I personally aspire.

A CHANGE IN THE 1930S

Perhaps you will allow me to begin with a little bit of history which is within my own cognizance and which has not hitherto been publicly revealed. I do not know that I could document it, but my memory of the circumstances is tolerably clear. I said in my last lecture that the monthly journal *Theology* was started in 1920 as an organ of the Cambridge school of Liberal Catholicism, though it was not advertised as such. It was edited until 1933 by E. G. Selwyn, and there was no doubt about what it stood for during that period. Selwyn resigned the editorship at the end of 1933 owing to pressure of other work, and was succeeded by S. C. Carpenter, Master of the Temple and afterwards Dean of Exeter. Carpenter was my own Tutor at Cambridge and I hold him in much affection and esteem. He was certainly a Liberal Catholic though he was not so closely associated with the Cambridge school, nor had he contributed to *Essays Catholic and Critical*. As editor of *Theology* he showed a facility for writing charming and enlightening editorials, which I have often envied and have never been able myself to compass. But otherwise he was hardly a good or at least an efficient editor. He had a habit of leaving bundles of MSS in railway trains and things like that. When I was asked to succeed him, I did not receive any technical apparatus or information from him about how to discharge my duties: I fancy he did it all out of his own head and in his own amateur way. However, that is by the way.

The point I wish to make is that I happen to know that in 1938 it was at the instigation of Sir Will Spens that I was invited to edit *Theology*, because he regarded me as a rather promising young member of the Cambridge school of Liberal Catholicism. I accepted the invitation, but in doing so I made it clear to the proprietors that I did not intend to continue *Theology* as an organ of that school of thought. I intended to broaden its basis and to try to make it a forum in which new developments in theology, especially in anglican theology, could find expression and, as it were, stimulate and fertilize one another. I believe that Spens, who was a canny Scot and a master in diplomacy, was at the time not at all pleased with this unforeseen outcome of his manoeuvre, especially as I also decided to leave Cambridge and move to St Deiniol's Library, Hawarden, where I was unlikely to be within easy reach of what he would regard as the most advantageous influences.

I mention this episode because it is evidence that I was

then aware that changes were taking place, or had taken place, in the theological climate which ought to be reflected in a journal like *Theology*. But I should add that I was not able then, and I am not able now, to state with any great precision or clarity what those changes were. I remember that in the early years of my editorship some readers used to complain that they could not make out what *Theology* now stood for: and I took this as a compliment rather than the reverse! But I also remember saying that, so far as anglicanism was concerned, the familiar parties or schools of thought—anglo-catholicism, evangelicalism, and modern or broad churchmanship, with their various wings—had all had their day and served their turn, and that we were ripe for the emergence of something new and synthetic, which would cut across them all.

Another and weightier piece of evidence that such a change had taken place may be seen in William Temple's introduction to the Report of the Archbishop's Commission on Christian Doctrine which made its report in 1938 but had started its work fifteen years before. In his introduction to the report (which was entitled *Doctrine in the Church of England*, and which has not, I think, received so much consideration as it merited) Temple said this:

If we began our work again today, its perspectives would be different. . . .

I am conscious of a certain transition of interest in our minds, as in the minds of theologians all over the world. . . .

If the security of the nineteenth century, already shattered in Europe, finally crumbles away in our country, we shall be pressed more and more towards a theology of Redemption. . . .

A theology of Redemption . . . tends . . . to sound the prophetic note; it is more ready to admit that much in this evil world is irrational and strictly unintelligible. . . .

We shall be coming closer to the New Testament. We have been learning again how impotent man is to save himself, how deep and pervasive is that corruption which theologians call Original Sin. Man needs above all else to be saved from himself. This must be the work of Divine Grace (pp. 16f.).

But it is time that I said what I mean by 'Neo-Orthodoxy'. I am not however going to answer that question by itself. There is in fact a considerable number of titles that I might have selected for this lecture in order to indicate what was new in the theological climate in the late 1930s—new, that is to say, so far as England was concerned.

'Neo-Orthodoxy' indicates that there were signs of a return to what its proponents regarded as a more orthodox way of defending the Christian religion in comparison with that which had been dominant in what they called 'the age of liberalism', but it was not a straightforward—or straight backward—resuscitation of *traditional* orthodoxy.

I might have entitled this lecture 'a theology of the Word of God'—a theology that seeks to be controlled by what God has said, as the Scriptures witness, instead of by what man has thought. That is to say, a theology that contrasted itself with that which stemmed from Schleiermacher, which was based on the religious consciousness or on man's religious experience, or from Ritschl, which was based on the moral impression made on believers by the Jesus of history, which contrasted itself also with those theological fashions which have been the subject of my three previous lectures.

Or again I might have entitled this lecture 'a theology of crisis', which would mean that the theology of this period was more patently related to a world in turmoil than to a world where peace and progress could be depended on—but it was also a theology of crisis because of its emphasis on the divine judgment which always hangs over man's best efforts.

Or I might have spoken of 'a dialectical theology', which would not signify the steady Hegelian rhythm of thesis, antithesis and synthesis, but which was dialectical in the sense of being a way of thinking that, instead of smoothly arguing from premises to a conclusion, proceeds by setting ideas in conflict and collision . . . by saying a Yes in one breath and a No in the next. It was, I mean, a type of theology that was dialectical, not in the Hegelian sense of unfolding an immanent process that was working itself out in the course of history, but in the sense that no syntheses are possible in history. Theological thought is always bound to be paradoxical and non-rational.

KARL BARTH AND THE WORD OF GOD

Now of course in this area and in this period the great name is that of Karl Barth. I hesitate to say anything about him here, for two reasons: first because I assume that all divines in Scotland know much more about him than I do; and secondly because I have to confess that I have read only a small portion of his voluminous works. Yet, though I am having in these lectures to ignore many important figures in 20th century theology, it would be intolerable to say nothing about Barth. But what am I to say?

I decided that you might perceive my estimate of his greatness as a theologian and at the same time my limitations in speaking of him, if I told you more or less what I said when I was asked, not long ago, to address one of our English so-called public schools on the subject of 'Karl Barth as a theologian'. A school audience is a taxing one at the best of times, and with such a subject I felt I had been given a pretty stiff assignment. My address was one of a course of four: other speakers were given other theologians to speak about, one of whom was Charles Gore.

I sought to get the school's attention by telling them an anecdote about Pope Pius IX. It was a witty remark he made about the four English statesmen with whom he had had to do: 'I like (he said) but I do not understand Mr Gladstone; Mr Cardwell I understand, but I do not like; I both like and understand Lord Clarendon; the Duke of Argyll I neither understand nor like.'

Then I explained that, when I had been asked to speak

about one of the four theologians whom they were hearing about, I had wondered whether I could adapt Pio Nono's saying to the selected four. I said I could not altogether, but that I would say of Charles Gore—whom I well remember and who was certainly a great man—I would say of him 'I understand him, but I do not like him'—that is to say, as a theologian. Whereas of another and a greater Charles—Karl Barth—I would say that 'I do not understand him, but I like him'.

I do not understand him, but I know he disturbs my mind, stretches it, sends it into a turmoil, shakes me up—which is what I think theologians ought to do, but which English theologians very seldom do. I might indeed say that Karl Barth reduces me to a salutary silence, but I suppose I must not allow him to do that at this moment! What I mean is that Karl Barth, more than anyone else I know, makes me aware that theologians and preachers, and all of us, who prattle away so easily about God, ought to be silent, if God is in truth the Ineffable Mystery, the *Mysterium Tremendum*, the Ground of all Being, the Final Arbiter of all Existence. If God be God, then all the earth ought to keep silent before him. And if in the silence we listened, perhaps we should hear what we shall never hear so long as we go on chattering away about religion and morality, and this and that, and one thing and another.

However, I said, I must tell you something about Karl Barth (remember, it was safe to assume that the boys knew practically nothing about him). He is a German-speaking Swiss, born in 1886, the son of a theological professor, so that he had theology in his bones, poor man! He studied under the leading professors of the time, that is, in the period before 1914; and Germany was then, as it is now, the principal home and factory of Protestant theology as of many other things too. That is where new fashions of thought are most often started.

The way of thinking that was fashionable in Germany,

and indeed elsewhere too, before 1914, was one of sunny confidence that man, at any rate western man, was steadily advancing in civilization and culture. Man's limitless capacity for achieving beauty, for attaining to truth, for diffusing goodness, was becoming more and more evident. Religion—Christianity, in particular[1]—endorsed, under-pinned, crowned this splendid confidence that what you might call the kingdom of heaven was in process of being built up on earth.

This way of thinking and of feeling was generally in the air before 1914, at any rate among high-minded men, and the theologians, at whose feet Karl Barth had sat, had main-tained that these beliefs and hopes of modern man were just what Jesus Christ had taught, but that, unfortunately, the simplicity and charm of his teaching had been obscured by having a lot of elaborate dogmas imposed upon it and by being organized into a great quasi-political church. But now the time had come when all that could be cleared away, so that the simple message of the fatherhood of God and the brotherhood of man would be able to exert untramelled its beautiful and beneficent influence in the world.

It was on such a world, so confident of its own powers and virtues and prospects, that the catastrophe of war broke in 1914. Karl Barth was at that time pastor of a country parish on the borders of Switzerland within hearing of the gun-fire in Alsace. The barbarism that had suddenly descended on the civilized world, and by which his own little country was surrounded, gave him furiously to think. Had he no better message for his people, in a world gone mad, than more smooth talk about man's capacities for peace and pro-gress? Had he no better Christ to preach than an amiable prophet of ineffective goodwill?

As Barth wrestled with these questions, he started to read

[1] For examples of the ways in which Jesus was pictured as 'the ideal modern man', see *Religious Thought in the Last Quarter-century*, edited by G. B. Smith (Chicago, 1927), pp. 31f.

the Bible with fresh eyes, and not only the Bible. He also read some of the great Christian authors who had taken a sombre view of the world and who had had a tragic sense of man's plight—Augustine, Luther, Calvin and (in the 19th century) Kierkegaard and Dostoievsky. The result was that by the end of the first World War Barth was ready to write a book which, when it was published, was described as a bomb dropped on the playground of the theologians. It was in the form of a book on the Epistle to the Romans: but on page after page it dealt out passionate and explosive paradoxes, which challenged the easy-going, optimistic Christianity that had been so popular—the Christianity that imagined that it had got God and Christ safely fixed and nicely understood.

Here, for example, are just a few sentences that Barth wrote about Christ:

> In Jesus, God becomes veritably a secret: He is made known as the Unknown, speaking in eternal silence; He protects himself from every intimate companionship and from all the impertinence of religion. He becomes a scandal to the Jews and to the Greeks foolishness (p. 98).

It was not, Barth said, for Christian preachers to boost man's wonderful capacities and achievements, but on the contrary to drive home man's frailty and folly and ignorance and guilt—and the absurdity of human pride. And then, when men had taken in the precariousness and the perils of their existence, then the preacher could proclaim the Word of God which comes from beyond the horizons of this world, and which can be heard only by men who know that they are hopelessly lost . . . hopelessly lost, unless there be a God who can find them, and freely set them right, and give them a new kind of life and power to love.

This was Barth's message, expressed with burning conviction. It had quite a different ring from all the Liberal Protestant preaching that was so familiar. When the book came out, it caused a great sensation in Germany, arousing both enthusiasm and hostility. Barth said later that he felt like a little urchin who had got up into the belfry of his parish church when everyone was asleep, and had just pulled a cord at random—only to find that he had set the great bell in motion: and in fear and trembling he realized that he had woken up not only his own household but the whole parish.

Here anyhow was a writer, a preacher, whom you could not just brush aside as one who went on droning out the dreary old platitudes of the pulpit. There was fire in this man's belly. There was thunder and lightning in his words. He made you tremble, and gasp, and hope, and adore. Not that he fiddled about with your emotions or tricked you with rhetoric. No, he was in deadly earnest and profoundly solemn, and extremely demanding.

And ever since that time, Karl Barth has been having that kind of effect on people. He was a Professor in Germany till Hitler expelled him. It was he more than anyone else who nerved the Church in Germany, the so-called Confessing Church, to resist the attempt of Hitler to nazify Christianity. Multitudes of Germans were seduced by that Nazi enterprise.

Then again in the second World War it was Karl Barth who inspired the Christians in the countries that were overrun by the Nazis to resist. He wrote a number of open letters to the Christians in the different countries—letters which, I should say, really deserve to be put alongside the Epistles in the New Testament, and which it might be even more worth while to study now. I was myself instrumental in persuading Barth to write such a letter to the Christians of Great Britain in 1941. It was published in a series of booklets that I edited during the war. In this letter, Barth put some pretty searching questions to the Christians of Great Britain. You claim, he said, to be fighting for 'Western civilization', 'the infinite value of the human personality', 'the brotherhood of man', and similar general ideas. But there is nothing distinctively Christian in those ideas, he said; they can be, and they have been, interpreted in all sorts of ways; they can be made to mean all sorts of things. You are on firm ground, Barth said, only when your allegiance is given clearly and unequivocally to Jesus Christ—to the Word of God instead of to the faltering and ambiguous words of man.

I am not sure that I agree with Barth about this. That is why I said that I like him but I do not understand him. I like him because he makes me think so hard, because he insists that I make up my mind what I really do believe, and for what I am prepared to stand up at whatever cost: and that is the most vital of questions.

But I do not claim to understand him, probably because I do not have his overpowering sense of the reality and all-sufficiency of what he calls 'the Word of God', by which he does not mean the Bible interpreted fundamentalistically, but a living, winning, overwhelming Voice which the Holy Ghost can enable us to hear if only we will be humble enough to listen.

BIBLICAL THEOLOGY IN ENGLAND

Pardon my simplicity. I have tried by this means to convey something of the reaction from liberalism in theology which in those days swept many people off their feet—or brought them to their knees in a way they had not been brought before. But in England—I do not say, in Britain—the impact of this reaction against liberalism, the impact of this challenge to all the common or garden defences of the Christian religion, was long delayed and never had the kind of devastating effect that it had elsewhere.

In so far as the theology of the Word of God or of crisis, or whatever you call it, did make an impact on our English theological schools or upon our clergy, I should say that it was more through the writings of Emil Brunner than of Karl Barth, and for a number of reasons. For one thing, some of Brunner's major works—notably *The Mediator* and *The Divine Imperative*—were earlier translated into English. Then, Brunner's writings are less formidably voluminous than Barth's. Dr Mascall, who was a mathematician before he became a theologian, has calculated that the probable length of Barth's *Dogmatics*, which is still in course of publication, will be about four million words. I fancy that many theological readers in England have been put off from reading Barth by the sheer amount of time and labour required for the purpose, and Barth insists, not unreasonably, that you must read him as a whole if you are to do justice to his thought. Brunner is more manageable in this respect and makes less exacting demands.

But a more revealing reason why the English took more readily to Brunner than to Barth is that his theology is less blatantly paradoxical, altogether less extreme and less extravagant in its assertions. If Barth is an Elijah, Brunner is an Elisha. And the English like their theology, as well as their politics, to be moderate: pink rather than red; 'both-and' rather than 'either-or'. They do not take easily to a 'dialectical' theology, or to a theology which says hard things about the use of reason. It seems too contrary to common sense. Nevertheless, there can be hardly any doubt that Barth is much the greater theologian, and if the English had brought themselves to grapple with Barth rather than with Brunner, they would have had their minds more fruitfully disturbed and stretched, whatever they might have made of it all in the end. Reading Brunner does not go to one's head in the same way: it is like having the whiskey of dialectical theology much diluted with water.

All the same, reading Brunner had its effect on the presentation of the Gospel by some of our English preachers, even if their auditories did not take kindly to the consequences. I remember a well-known and distinguished English clergyman, who ministered to a congregation of highly educated people, telling me that his pulpit message had been like that of, say, *Reality*, a book by B. H. Streeter, one of the most engaging of liberal theologians—and his congregation liked it well. But then my friend read Brunner's *The Mediator*, and it at once changed the character of his preaching, with the result that his congregation did not like it at all and used to say to him 'Why have your sermons become so queer and unintelligible?'

But Barth did make some impact in England, well before the second World War, principally through Sir Edwyn Hoskyns (1884-1937), whom I mentioned in my last lecture. Hoskyns was primarily a New Testament scholar—a New Testament theologian, which is not necessarily the same thing. In the early 1920s he used to expound the New Testament from the standpoint of the Catholic Modernists and the Liberal Catholics. 'The religion of the New Testament had authority because it came out of a unique religious experience—the religious experience of the primitive Church.'[1] But in 1924 or 1925 he read Karl Barth's *Epistle to the Romans*, and this seems to have been a turning-point. Thereafter he spoke less and less about religious experience and more and more about revelation. Also we find him increasingly using the paradoxical modes of speech which he seems to have picked up from Barth. His superb English translation of Barth's *Romans* appeared in 1933: the work of translating it no doubt affected—some would say, infected—his own style.

While I knew Hoskyns, I did not know him at all well, and I never heard him lecture. But I knew many of his pupils as well as undergraduates who attended his lectures. He certainly elicited in his pupils a passionate concern about the importance of theology and at the same time he was insistent on a rigorous use of critical methods. My recollection is that those who attended his lectures in the 1930s reacted in different ways. Many derived from them an unforgettable stimulus to theological seriousness and a sense

[1] J. O. Cobham in *Cambridge Sermons* by E. C. Hoskyns (1938), p. xvi.

of the overwhelming importance of the New Testament, but others were impatient with his manner of talking. I remember one undergraduate—who was by no means stupid or obtuse—telling me that he and his friends used to occupy themselves during Hoskyns' lectures in counting the number of times he used his favourite clichés, which were what would be vulgarly called 'Barthian' clichés. But it would be an injustice both to Barth and to Hoskyns to say that Hoskyns was a 'Barthian'. He did however more than anyone else in England—or at least in the Church of England —regard Barth as the prophet for that time.

The letter which Hoskyns addressed to Barth in 1936, and which is printed as an appendix to his *Cambridge Sermons*, indicates what he considered he owed to Barth. There is not time to read it all, but I will read just one paragraph :

> For us, as for you in Central Europe, the subject-matter of the Bible is difficult, strange and foreign. Yet in our aloofness we know that its relevance lies in its strangeness, and that we are involved in its definition of human life. What you have written has enabled a large number of men and women in England to see this tension of far and near, this contradiction of strangeness and relevance, more clearly, and to recognize its vast importance (p. 219).

During these years Hoskyns was also much affected by Kittel's *Wörterbuch* and he became absorbed in the extraordinary significance of biblical words and language. But his main work, I suppose, was to advance the claim that, if the critical study of the New Testament, and of the synoptic gospels in particular, is pressed to its conclusion what you came up against was a fully supernatural Christ—and not the Jesus of Liberal Protestantism nor the kind of development which was the thesis of Catholic Modernism. There was no breach or incompatibility between the Gospel and the Church. This was already the theme of his contribution to *Essays Catholic and Critical* on 'The Christ of the Synoptic Gospels' and it was elaborated in his book *The Riddle of the New Testament*,[1] of which, incidentally, I remember presenting a copy to M. Loisy, but he never told me what he thought of it.

Hoskyns, through his lecturing and preaching and writing and not least through his pupils, undoubtedly had a considerable influence, though I must say I think it is somewhat exaggerated in the memoir by Charles Smyth which is prefixed to *Cambridge Sermons*. I am sure that Hoskyns' influence was in the main very salutary, but it had also a less fortunate side. This leads me to say something about the enthusiasm for 'biblical theology' of which in England he must be accounted one of the founding fathers. 'Biblical theology' is in fact one of the elements in the complex of trends which I am grouping together under the title 'Neo-Orthodoxy'. There is of course a broad sense in which all Christian theology is biblical, but the kind of 'biblical theology' which came to be cultivated, and became fashionable, in the 1940s and 1950s had a special character.

In the first place, it arose from a suspicion—nay, a conviction—that theologians both ancient and modern had been prone to interpret the Bible in terms of their own thought-forms and to read into the Bible ideas which were derived from other and later sources. Dogmatic theologians, for example, had looked at the Bible through the spectacles of their own dogmatic systems and had found there what they wanted to find. 'The Church to teach, the Bible to prove.' Or again the Liberal Protestants had sought and found in the Bible, or at any rate in the alleged kernel of its message, only what was congenial to a modern humanitarian. And so on.

Now the biblical theologians maintained that the right course was to try, as far as possible, so to get inside the minds of the biblical writers as to be able to explain their meaning without importing into it later prepossessions or interests.

[1] Written in collaboration with Noel Davey; published in 1931.

Further, they maintained that, if you did this, and succeeded, so to speak, in hearing what the Word of God in the Bible had to say for itself, then you would also find that it had something startling and unexpected and highly illuminating to say to us in our contemporary situation. Hoskyns himself was a master in the art of this kind of biblical exposition. So far, so good.

The general impression given was that there is a biblical world-view which is the only authentically Christian world-view, and that it was the proper task of Christian preachers and teachers to think themselves into that world-view, to expose its implications however strange they might be, and bring all theological ideas and doctrines to this judgment-seat. Whereas many modern preachers had been wont to base their discourses on some contemporary question and then to work or refer back to the Bible to illustrate, to eluci-date, or to enforce their point (but not only to the Bible), the biblical theologians held that all proper preaching must be based on the exegesis of the biblical text and proceed from the Bible. This was well enough in the hands of a master of biblical exegesis equipped with all the various kinds of knowledge required, but few preachers are so equipped, and they are more likely to be able to speak with conviction and authority if they start from the contemporary knowledge that they more or less share with those whom they are addressing. I am drawing only a rough distinction, but I hope my point is clear.

Another disadvantage of this biblical theology was that the ambition to get right inside the biblical world-view made its adepts talk a language and use forms of thought which were largely unintelligible to their hearers and too remote from the furniture of their minds for any communication to take place. Preachers, when they were apprised of this fact, were inclined to ease their consciences with the notion that communication of the Gospel can take place only by the miraculous operation of the Holy Ghost, who bloweth where he listeth, and so it is not within their power to do anything much about it. Thus an effect of the fashionable preoccupation with biblical theology was to make those who fell for it less and less able to communicate with ordinary people. They tended to become a coterie of initiates.

Then, it came about that the biblical-theology movement, where it was open to be disturbed, was fatally wounded by the claim that the biblical world-view must be demythologized if the Gospel is to get across to the world of the present day.

And it was already a grave weakness that the assumption that all good theology must be biblical was calculated to encourage devaluation of what has happened in the development of Christian thought and life after the New Testament period, and especially to a depreciation of modern theology which, by those who glibly claimed to be post-critical or post-liberal, was treated with an unwarranted neglect, not to say contempt.[1] The truth, I believe, is that the great questions as regards traditional Christianity which had been raised during the so-called liberal period may not have been satisfactorily answered, but they still remained to be answered, and were not to be short-circuited by magnifying the availability of the Bible by itself as the text-book of the Christian faith. What I have been trying to say is that mixed up in the fashion of biblical theology, as a mode of defending the Christian religion, were both salutary and noxious elements.

For my part, I owe to it an appreciation of the insight that can come to individuals and to groups of people who set themselves, with adequate knowledge or guidance, to discover what the biblical writings were really saying in their original *milieu*, and then go on to ask what (if any-

[1] Cp. what Bonhoeffer says in his *Letters and Papers from Prison*, p. 62: 'There are so few nowadays who have any real interest or sympathy for the nineteenth century. . . . Hardly anyone has the slightest idea what was achieved during the last century by our own grandfathers. How much of what they knew has already been forgotten!'

thing) they can mean for us today. The qualifying words 'if anything' are important. Those biblical theologians, who supposed that there must be a meaning of permanent value everywhere in the Bible, found themselves carrying typological exegesis to fantastic lengths, and also their philology was insufficiently critical.

ON TO ORTHODOXY

The writer who made the biggest dent in my own thinking in the 1930s was Reinhold Niebuhr. While there are undoubted affinities between his way of thinking and the theology of crisis and also biblical theology, Niebuhr stands apart, and he got under my skin more than any of the other critics of theological liberalism.

This was partly because, in the concern I had always had about the social implications of the Christian faith, I was convicted by Niebuhr of having made the mistake of taking those implications to be idealistic, utopian and perfectionist. I saw that this resulted from not taking into account the truth that is enshrined in the traditional dogma known as 'original sin'. But Niebuhr did more than this. He showed, through his comment on current affairs and his analysis of social and political movements, that in the traditional doctrines, notably that of justification by faith, there were resources for illuminating secular conflicts and problems, resources of which I had been hitherto unaware and which had formed no part of what I had understood by Liberal Catholicism, though I do not say that they were incompatible with it.

But instead of enlarging upon that, I am going now to say something about a man who was, to a considerable extent, a British counterpart of Reinhold Niebuhr: I mean, D. R. Davies (1889-1958).[1] His book *On to Orthodoxy* (1939), as its

[1] His autobiography, *In Search of Myself*, was published posthumously in 1961.

title suggests, could provide a wealth of documentation for this lecture.

D. R. Davies was the son of a Welsh miner, and he himself started working down the pit before he was thirteen. His experience of poverty and deprivation of opportunity turned him into an ardent socialist and trade unionist. At the age of sixteen he was on the local executive of the South Wales Miners' Federation. He was a member of the Independent Labour Party when it was inspired by a religious fervour under Keir Hardie's leadership. Davies became a voracious reader. He had a fine intelligence, a keen imagination, and a flair for effective rhetoric. At length, after many hazards and setbacks, he was ordained as a Congregational minister. The Christianity which now appealed to him and which he preached was not the calvinistic orthodoxy of his home. It was an unvarnished version of Liberal Protestantism or what he called, in *On to Orthodoxy*, 'Christian Liberalism'. I do not think he had any knowledge of, or contact with, Catholic Modernism or Liberal Catholicism. In *On to Orthodoxy* he writes:

> My mind goes back to my student days—days of azure optimism. We bowed down in reverence before German scholarship and theological learning. That magnificent tradition of New Testament Criticism stretched from Otto Bauer down to Strauss, Pfleiderer, Marburg [*sic*], Hermann and Harnack and Deismann [*sic*] . . . (p. 52).

But he was really less concerned about New Testament criticism than about the social gospel which he lapped up from such writers as Francis Peabody and Walter Rauschenbusch. Thus again in *On to Orthodoxy* he writes:

> From those early days in South Wales (1906 *circa*) down to a few years ago, I was closely identified with the Socialist Movement. When I became a minister, as I did in 1917, it was largely in the belief and faith that Christianity was the true Socialism, and that the Church must be won for the Social

Gospel. . . . In good faith, I identified my Christianity with my Socialist politics. I am still of the opinion that if the interpretation of religion made by Christian Liberalism is correct, there was nothing unreasonable in identifying Christianity with Socialism (pp. 107f.).

In the course of his pilgrimage—for Davies was a natural pilgrim, and an adventurer in the best sense of the word—he became a pacifist, and later a marxist. He turned his Congregational Church into a Labour Church. He was elected as a municipal councillor (he was now working in England) and stood as a candidate for parliament. He was an accomplished orator and a popular speaker for all the causes he embraced. He was an idealist and a perfectionist. But in between the wars his confidence in man's powers to establish a socialist utopia was gradually shaken and sapped and finally dissolved. At last he became completely disillusioned about the possibility of realizing the ideals which had been his inspiration. He abandoned the ministry of the Church, and went through an experience of black despair.

He was an intense and well-informed student of what was happening in Europe in the 1930s; he was, for instance, in Spain during the civil war. His sombre reactions to what was happening in the world were compounded with his own personal problems. Of this period he writes:

As the significance of each group . . . of events became clear to my mind, my whole being underwent a most painful process of disintegration. I became oppressed with a dreadful sense of futility. As I came to realize the failure to establish peace; as the utter irrationality of the whole economic life of Europe broke in upon me; as the meaning of Fascism gradually dawned upon me; and finally, as the illusion of Russia broke in upon me, I suffered a despair I had never previously known (p. 61).

It was now that he experienced a profound conversion to Christian orthodoxy, by which he meant, he says, 'not . . .

D

the officially accepted Creeds and confessions of the Church so much as the substantive experience and knowledge that are proclaimed in those Creeds' (p. 112).

It seemed to him that the Christian Liberalism which had determined his faith before, and by which generations of Christians had been led astray, had had four fatal consequences:

(1) A false estimation of human nature.
(2) The practical banishment of the otherworldly element in Christian Ethic.
(3) The denial of the uniqueness of Christianity.
(4) The secularisation of life and religion (p. 13).

As regards his own recovered faith (or rather it came to him as an altogether new faith) he sums it up at the end of *On to Orthodoxy* in a *confessio fidei* with ten articles. I will take leave to reproduce them because they constitute a very direct and pretty comprehensive illustration of the Neo-Orthodoxy of that time.

(1) I believe that man is radically evil, that sin is of the very texture of human nature.

(2) I believe that, owing to that original, inherent sin, man is incapable of creating a just society (to say nothing of a perfect society); that he is cursed with a fatal contradiction which ordains that the power by which he advances in civilisation nullifies and destroys his progress.

(3) I believe that, if left to his own resources, man is doomed to destruction and History is fated to disintegrate.

(4) I believe that History, however, will find its fulfilment in a world beyond death, because it is the working out of the will of God who is preparing man for the Kingdom of God.

(5) I believe that that Kingdom enters into History through Christ who endows man with the power to overcome the contradiction of his being, and thus forgives him his sin.

(6) I believe that the process of forgiveness to the individual person in time comes to fulfilment in eternity in the perfect society, known as the Kingdom of God.

(7) I believe that all History, therefore, is under the will of a Transcendent, Omnipotent, Creative, Judging and Redeeming God, who has come into History in Christ and through His Cross and Resurrection initiates the coming of the Kingdom in the hearts of men.

(8) I believe that that same Christ will appear again in History to effect the Final Judgment which will be the end of time.

(9) I believe that the Church is the agent of God in the world to continue the redeeming, transcendent love of God among men.

(10) I believe that the supreme task of the Church, therefore, is to preach the redeeming grace of God and bring man to repentance, to which task all else must be subordinate (pp. 207f.).

In all his subsequent writings Davies reiterated, elaborated and to some extent refined these articles of his belief.

I read *On to Orthodoxy* when it was first published, with a good deal of excitement. It seemed to drive home the lessons I had been learning from Reinhold Niebuhr, and it did so in terms of British rather than American experience. I re-read *On to Orthodoxy* in preparation for these lectures, and it strikes me still as a powerful piece of writing, and one that reveals not only the experience of Davies himself but of many who at that time were, as you may say, converted from Christian Liberalism to Neo-Orthodoxy. Davies has a vivid, pungent, racy style: there is never a dull page. He was a Celt and was given to making bold generalizations which offended more scrupulous minds: I remember that they both fascinated me and left me suspicious. It would be a mistake to suppose that there was not a very penetrating intelligence behind them. He tended of course to caricature the 'Christian Liberalism' against which he was now in revolt. But he knew what he was about, and believed that his contemporaries would not be woken up to the truth about the human situation by academic niceties or carefully qualified argumentation. He was a born preacher.

Soon after reading *On to Orthodoxy* I got to know Davies personally and we became intimate friends. He came to St Deiniol's Library, Hawarden, of which I was then Warden, in order to prepare for ordination by Archbishop William Temple into the ministry of the Church of England. For some years Davies greatly affected my outlook and my thinking, as is shown in one or two of the books which I published at that time. We remained devoted friends until his death, and I am conscious of an undying debt to him; but after a few years I came to have increasing misgivings about his preoccupation with original sin. He seemed to have an almost one-track obsession with the subject. At that time, the teaching of F. D. Maurice was making a big impact on my mind. It challenged the notion that the Gospel must be proclaimed and accepted as bad news *before* it can be proclaimed as good news. Nevertheless, I should still say that Davies was a prophet for his time.

There were those who thought and said that the various trends and tendencies which I have grouped together as 'Neo-Orthodoxy' were a *pathological*[1] Christian response to the abnormal and diseased condition of the world in that period when Nazism and Fascism seemed to be triumphing. I would not deny that there is something in that, but I would also say that the theologians of crisis had rediscovered aspects, and more than aspects, of what is involved in biblical and traditional Christianity. But as we have seen there were others, like Tyrrell and Figgis, who had made this rediscovery and witnessed to it earlier in the century. Periods and fashions are seldom so sharply distinguishable from one another as lecturers and authors are pleased to make out.

[1] E.g. see C. E. Raven, *Good News of God* (1943), p. 6.

5

Christian Radicalism

As we come nearer to the contemporary scene, it becomes more difficult—for me, at any rate—clearly to identify any one fashion, mood, school or train of thought as characteristic of the period, and *a fortiori* to find a satisfactory title to denote it. I have taken the title 'Christian Radicalism' from the essay by Mr David Edwards on 'A New Stirring in English Christianity' in *The Honest to God Debate*. But, even more than in the case of 'Neo-Orthodoxy', I use the title only as a convenient way of indicating a variety of trends or tendencies. I am not yet sure whether one can claim any particular coherence for them. They may, or they may not, as time goes on, exhibit a plainer common direction than is apparent at present.

This lecture will, therefore, be even more impressionistic than its predecessors. I propose, first of all, to notice some of the things that have happened during these last few years, especially those within my own direct acquaintance, and to offer some reflections upon them, and then to draw some distinctions, and finally to indicate my own present disposition.

SOUNDINGS AND OBJECTIONS

I should say that in England 'Neo-Orthodoxy' was the predominant fashion in theology during the second World War and the following decade. Neo-Orthodoxy in the form of 'biblical theology' encouraged a frame of mind in which the foundations of theology—above all, the reality of God—were assumed to be secure and one could work confidently away at describing and perhaps repairing or refashioning the superstructure.

There was a rapid increase of interest in the ecumenical movement and questions about church unity. Liturgiology was studied, and questions about the forms and implications of worship were eagerly canvassed. The so-called 'problem of communication' began to be discussed. There was thought not to be much doubt about *what* ought to be communicated—the substance of biblical theology: the question was *how* to communicate it. I found this state of affairs reflected in my experience as editor of *Theology*, both in the range of articles that was submitted to me and in the topics that would stir up controversy and elicit many letters to the editor. Episcopacy was a never-failing subject of interest, and baptism, and matters of ecclesiastical organization or reorganization: all of them subjects of subordinate importance compared with those that had agitated the minds of the men who were concerned about the defence of the Christian religion earlier in the century. I am sure that there were more exceptions to this generalization than I recollect, but by and large it is the impression that was left on my mind.

As I am now being unashamedly personal, I will also recall that often during those years I used to say to my friends that I was disconcerted by the fact that theological students, the younger clergy and the like, when I conversed with them, never seemed to shock me by coming out with any startling novelties or disturbing thoughts: on the contrary, I could shock them by the things I said much more than they ever shocked me by anything they said. It should have been the other way on, as I was now a fuddy-duddy who should be allergic to new ideas. I found much more openness to the need for some fresh and fundamental theological thinking among the laymen of the Christian Frontier Council (of which I was acting as secretary at the time) than I did in professionally theological or ecclesiastical circles.

However, it was not the case that there was no thinking about basic questions going on anywhere. The writings (or some of them) of what I may call post-neo-orthodox theologians like Rudolf Bultmann and Paul Tillich were already available and were read by a few. Martin Buber's *I and Thou* and its sequels had struck deep into the thinking of quite a number of Christian minds. There were here and there in England philosophical theologians who were grappling with the searching questions that had been posed by linguistic analysis about the meaning or meaninglessness of theological statements. Or again Dietrich Bonhoeffer's *Letters and Papers from Prison* made something of an impact when they first appeared in 1953. But none of this seemed to make much difference to our English theological climate. That is my impression. I should agree with a writer in the July 1963 issue of *The Hibbert Journal* who said :

> In recent years . . . the English theological tradition has been very conventional. The ghosts of philosophical Idealism, and of common-sense rationalism, still hang over it. An occasional skirmisher takes up existentialism, or logical empiricism, or some other philosophical fashion; but this is looked upon as a private oddity.

I need hardly say that a notable change has come over the scene during the last few years, which has made it appropriate to look for some new term, such as 'Christian Radicalism', to register it. But what has been happening is, I believe, too complicated and confused and inchoate to justify a contented use of any single term. I am accustomed to deprecate talk about 'the new theology', etc., since it may easily be taken to imply the emergence of something much more tangible and specifiable than I can yet perceive. We have not to do with anything so recognizable as 'the new theology' of R. J. Campbell.

Soon after I returned to Cambridge in 1956, some of the (more or less) younger theologians there, who (I was relieved to discover) felt much as I did about the lethargic or ostrich-like condition of English, or at least of anglican, theology, suggested that we might meet from time to time to share our disquiets, to see how far we agreed about what questions theologians ought now to be facing, and to interchange thought about the ways in which our own minds were working. The centenary was approaching of *Essays and Reviews*, the book which had had a very disturbing effect on English theology in what seemed to us a somewhat analogous situation (an effect comparable, I imagine, with that of the Robertson Smith case in Scotland). We were not so immodest as to suppose that, even if we eventually published anything, it would have a similar effect. As it was, some years elapsed before we decided to publish a volume of essays, and we should have been quite happy if some other group of theologians had anticipated us, and enabled us to ride off on the agreeable task of criticizing their essays!

The subjects of our essays were determined partly by our desire to direct attention to some fundamental questions which had not been receiving, during the period of which I was speaking just now, the attention which they called for, and partly by the interests and aptitudes of the members of our group which had not been constituted with a view to any systematic coverage. Thus we were not in a position to deal with all the questions we regarded as important.

We naturally gave some thought to the title of the volume, and our choice of *Soundings* was intended to be not only euphonious but significant. We took the view that there was a great deal of fresh exploratory work to be done in the region of fundamentals and that it would be misleading to disguise the fact that we had no new theological construction to propose. Our purpose was to ask questions rather than to answer them, though, as I noticed in the case of Édouard Le Roy,[1] the two exercises are seldom so separable as authors may wish to represent them to be, least of all when a number of authors are collaborating.

[1] See p. 51 above.

As regards the readers whom we hoped to reach, they included two classes. On the one hand, theologians and theological students to whom we wished to suggest what some of their agenda should be during the coming period; and on the other hand, lay people who had a potential interest in theology but who found that most theological books took too much for granted and so failed to speak to their condition. I do not think that we got on to the latter wave-length anything like so nearly as we aspired to do, though I remember being gratified when a lay professor told me, soon after *Soundings* had been published in the autumn of 1962, that he had just ordered a dozen copies to give to his lay friends as Christmas presents.

Soundings has in fact had much larger sales than we could reasonably have expected it to have, but we cannot put that down solely to whatever inherent merits it may be deemed to possess. For, soon after its publication, adventitious circumstances helped to provide it with a favourable market, though not necessarily with a favourable reception. *Soundings* got caught up in the excitement that was caused by some other quite unconnected events and publications, most of all by the Bishop of Woolwich's now famous *Honest to God*. But I will continue the story from my own point of view and with a further reference to Cambridge.

It happened that, in entire independence of *Soundings* and before ever it was published, the Divinity Faculty at Cambridge had projected for the following Lent term (1963) a course of four open lectures for members of the university on 'Fundamental Objections to Christian Belief'. Two of the lecturers happened to be contributors to *Soundings*, but that was accidental : there was no direct connexion between the two undertakings. These open lectures attracted surprisingly large audiences of undergraduates of about 1,500 each time. No one can be sure why they did so, but it is generally supposed that it struck the auditory as both unusual and welcome that Christian theologians should be showing their awareness of objections to their beliefs without at the same time supplying comforting answers to the objections. Through the pressing initiative of a publisher the lectures appeared in print very soon after their delivery was completed, and, although personally I do not rate the book at all highly, I must say it has had a very large circulation for a book of this kind, though of course its sales were to be dwarfed by those of *Honest to God*.

THE 1963 CONTROVERSIES

Honest to God was published at about the same time. Since its origins are now well known, I need not explain them, except that I would emphasize that this again was an entirely independent event. It is true that Dr Robinson was a Cambridge don before he became Bishop of Woolwich, but so far as I know what he says in *Honest to God* was not explicit in his mind before he left Cambridge. There is indeed a certain piquancy in recalling that he was still in Cambridge when we formed our *Soundings* group, and that we deliberately did not invite him to join us, since we took him to be an inveterate apostle of biblical theology and the liturgical movement—and a highly qualified and influential one at that.

Another book also was published at this time which attracted less attention but should be taken into account if we are talking about 'Christian Radicalism'. I mean *God Is No More* by Werner and Lotte Pelz. I found that undergraduates were more excited by this than by *Honest to God*, and I shall recur to it.

Other publications or public pronouncements added to the excitement as the months went on. A canon of Southwark Cathedral said something about the need for a new morality[1] which was taken up by the newspapers. Another, on his appointment there, protested against being required to

[1] See Douglas Rhymes, *Christian Personal Values and Sexual Morality* (1964).

assent to the Thirty-Nine Articles of Religion, though the sting of his protest was drawn by his assenting to them all the same. These utterances, together with the well-known adventurousness of the Bishop of Southwark and the Bishop of Woolwich's being his suffragan, led to talk about 'South-bank religion'—as a good or bad thing according to the point of view of the speaker.

For by now all these evidences of an unfamiliar ferment and openness to new ideas in the theological and ecclesiastical worlds were evoking strong reactions which ranged from rejoicing and relief to horror and amazement. These varied reactions could be liberally documented from the booklets and articles that have since been published, from the files of the religious press, or from the letters received by those of us who were regarded, rightly or wrongly, as being respon-sible for starting the commotion. There was plenty of the *odium theologicum* flying about, but more worth attending to were the expressions of hope, coming from many quarters, that there was going to be a new deal in the presentation of the Christian faith and a salutary upheaval in the Church. There are, for example, some moving illustrations of that hope in the letters addressed to the Bishop of Woolwich and published in *The Honest to God Debate*.

Before trying to disentangle the different strands in this affair, I want to say something about two separate matters.

First, the role of television, about which our earlier de-fenders of the faith did not have to worry themselves. It is a subject that should now have a place in any general con-sideration of the defence of the Christian religion. Televised discussions played quite a prominent part in the theological ferment about which I have been speaking, increasing the publicity of it and adding to the excitement.

I will make only a few personal comments. I have never myself sought access to a television studio, but it has seemed to me that, if one is asked to discuss through this medium things one has said in print, one should be prepared to do so unless one has an obvious *alibi*. But it is one thing to publish a book or an article in which one can carefully weigh one's words, though even then there is no telling just whom they may reach; it is another thing to engage in an impromptu conversational discussion which may be listened to and looked at by millions of people. Even if one were able to weigh one's words with the same care that one does when writing, it is inevitable that they will be often misunderstood or misinterpreted without there being any opportunity for subsequent explanation. Whatever service may be rendered to those who take your point, others will be scandalized or mystified whom you would not want to scandalize or mystify.

I do not see any way of avoiding this hazard except by refusing to engage in this kind of discussion. It is no use saying that one should eschew any remarks that may be hurtful and be careful to avoid giving offence. I am told by television viewers that it is easy to detect when a speaker is playing for safety or withholding or disguising what he really thinks, and that such apparent insincerity discredits him altogether. No doubt, different speakers have different conversational styles according to their temperaments. For my part, I have always regarded Arnold Bennett's maxim that 'in conversation you are not on oath' as a good one. I could not easily renounce it, even if I wanted to do so, in a television conversation, in which it is essential to be natural and spontaneous. I offer these reflections not as though they were a solution of what is admittedly a serious problem, but as an explanation of the willingness of some of us to expose ourselves, when invited to do so, to the hazards involved in saying what we think through this medium.

The second thing I want to say is that, although *Honest to God, Soundings, Objections to Christian Belief*, etc., may have set off this commotion (which for some reason chiefly originated in the Church of England), it is important to realize that there were previously or contemporaneously publications and events elsewhere which may prove to be of more permanent potency or consequence. I will give four examples.

(1) If I had not excused myself at the outset of these lectures from attending to the work of Scottish divines, I should want to bring in to any account of 'Christian Radicalism' Professor Gregor Smith's book, *The New Man: Christianity and Man's Coming of Age*, published in 1956. If I may say so without impertinence, I apprehend that that book is a more intrinsically valuable instance of radical Christian thought than others that have received more publicity. If Professor Gregor Smith had been a bishop (which, I grant, is hard to imagine) and if the gist of his theme had appeared on the front page of the *Observer* with an unsuitably sensational title, it might well have had the same effect as *Honest to God*.

(2) The posthumous publication in translation of Père Teilhard de Chardin's writings was already kindling a new theological interest in a good many minds—not only his bold exposition of a world-view that was both scientific and religious, but his pointers to a new type of Christian spirituality in *Le Milieu Divin*. (By the way, I remember Miss Maude Petre saying to me about 1940 that she considered Teilhard de Chardin was attempting to do what the Roman Catholic Modernists would have done if they had been permitted to continue their work. I expect that was the first time I heard of him.)

(3) Much more pregnant with possibilities has been the astonishing change of climate in the Roman Catholic Church, which has resulted from the initiative of Pope John XXIII. We know that in the past such changes have been all too easily reversible. But, so far as one can judge, a change has now taken place that is not going to be reversible, though it is much too soon to estimate what may come of it. It looks

as though dispersed through the Roman Catholic Church there were numerous groups and individuals, including cardinals and bishops, who were waiting, maybe unconsciously, for a moment of release from inhibitions, and who felt in their bones that the stone-walling defence of the Christian religion, which had become characteristic of their Church, was no longer tolerable. Pope John XXIII provided the moment of release.

When we consider not only the size and extension of the Roman Catholic Church, but the human and spiritual resources which it enfolds, there are evidently potentialities of renewal there to which no limit can be set, even if it is not to be expected that they will be realized otherwise than slowly. Alongside what may be germinating there, our little commotion in England may seem very provincial and not much more than a storm in a tea-cup. Nevertheless, it is important for us.

(4) To return then to England. I said that for some reason our commotion had chiefly originated in the Church of England, but it is certainly not confined there. For evidence that there is a similar ferment at work in other denominations it is enough to cite the report *Towards a Quaker View of Sex*, which again originated quite independently and is a sign of the reappraisal of traditional Christian attitudes that is going on far and wide.

GROWING POINTS

I suppose it is natural that, when a variety of independent outbreaks or manifestations of apparently new ways of thinking more or less synchronize, observers and publicists should be inclined to infer that they have a common origin, and that in places where they are disliked there should be talk of an insidious conspiracy. It is easier to denounce— or to applaud—things, however disparate, when they have been tied together and given a single label—much easier than to draw careful and judicious distinctions. So it has come about that we have had many references not only to 'the new theology' and 'Southbank religion', but also to 'Cambridge theology' and 'the Cambridge theologians'.

I should like to take this opportunity of pointing out that, as regards Cambridge, such talk is wide of the mark. In the first place, there are plenty of theologians in Cambridge—probably wiser than the rest of us—who have been in no way implicated in the publications to which some of us have recently set our hands, and it must be embarrassing for them to be credited or discredited with what they are not responsible for. In the second place, those of us who have been responsible for collaborating in publication all have minds of our own. We do not see eye to eye, I am thankful to say. We do not, and we do not wish to, stand for anything like a party line. I believe that what F. J. A. Hort wrote to a friend in 1879, when comparing Cambridge with Oxford, is still true of Cambridge:

> The way in which Churchmen of all opinions, both graduates and undergraduates, are accustomed to meet and work together . . . keeps party-spirit in check. . . . In this and other respects we have no sharply-defined camps, and consequently no need of prematurely closing the mind against growth in knowledge and experience.[1]

Still more is this *caveat* warranted with regard to the publications and initiatives that did not originate in Cambridge. When a correspondent of a weekly journal mentioned 'the Woolwich-Vidler group', I wrote to ask him what he meant since I did not know anything about it, but he had no satisfactory explanation to offer because there is none. Not that I should ever desire to dissociate myself from Dr Robinson where in fact we were associated. We have been good friends for many years. But, in this instance, I did not see or hear of *Honest to God* until it was in print.

[1] *Life and Letters of F. J. A. Hort* (1896), ii. 277.

It may seem that I am labouring this point unnecessarily, but if any one is to understand what for convenience I am calling 'Christian Radicalism', he must appreciate the independence and heterogeneity of its ingredients.

I come then to my attempt to distinguish or disentangle them, and I must hope that I shall not make confusion worse confounded. I am going to take some hints that were given in an article by Mr H. E. Root on 'What is the Gospel?' which appeared in the June 1963 number of *Theology*. He was reviewing a series of B.B.C. Third Programme broadcast talks. It struck me at the time as a very perceptive article, and it seems to be still more so now.

There is general agreement at present, as he says, that, since neither 'the imagery and mythology of first century Palestine' nor 'the thought forms of the Graeco-Roman world in which the gospel received its classical, doctrinal definition' are any longer ours, the gospel must be translated, restated or reinterpreted in such a way as to be intelligible today. The pressure of that need, we may say, was the starting-point of most, if not all, of the theologians whom I have been considering in these lectures, and we have seen the different routes by which they proceed from that starting-point. A question that has been there all the time, and has often become explicit, is: How are we to tell what is a genuine or authentic translation and what is not? As Root says, 'to translate one has to know the meaning or the substance of the thing one is translating'. He detects and distinguishes two divergent attitudes to this problem at the present time which, I should say, have had their parallels from the beginning of the century, and indeed before then. It may be that the divergence seems sharper now or perhaps simpler, but it is not new.

On the one hand, there are those who hold that the work of translation must never lose sight of what they believe to be the original or traditional or objective substance of the gospel, which affirms that a transcendent God has acted

decisively in history, above all in the life, death and resurrection of Jesus. This was, as we saw, precisely the contention of O. C. Quick and A. E. J. Rawlinson. This is what
they urged against what they regarded as inadequate transla-
tions. Thus Quick's main criticism of Liberal Protestantism
and Catholic Modernism was that

> somehow the orthodox Christian feels that the Being Whom
> he calls God has been left out of the intellectual constructions
> of both parties. . . .[1]

Again, Rawlinson, in his critique of Le Roy, argued that
the Gospel 'cannot possibly be independent of all imaginable
conclusions, either of historical science or of philosophical
speculation' and in particular, 'divorced from its basis in
history, must needs lose its essential power'.[2] The substance
of the Gospel is that God was in Christ reconciling the world
unto himself. Translate, reinterpret, demythologize or re-
mythologize as much as you like, provided you can still say
that.

I apprehend that most theologians—including probably
most theologians who are at present being called 'radicals'—
would say that, and further would agree with Rawlinson
that Christianity 'cannot possibly be independent of all
imaginable conclusions . . . of philosophical speculation'
or, to put the case more positively, that Christianity implies
a world-view and a metaphysic. They would say that, though
they may not be philosophical theologians themselves, there
is a proper and a necessary work for philosophical theologians to do, and that it is indispensable that there should still
be the equivalent of what used to be called 'natural theology'
or 'rational theology'. For, they would say, you cannot
expect to defend or to commend the Christian religion to
reasonable men unless you can show that there are reasonable
grounds for believing that the world is of such a character
that the assertions of the Gospel, e.g. that God was in Christ

[1] See p. 68 above.   [2] See pp. 77f. above.

reconciling the world unto himself, can make sense in it. All this leaves plenty of scope for translation and reinterpretation, for new essays in philosophical theology, and for beginning all over again.

On the other hand, there is a divergent way of conceiving of what needs to be done. There are those who would say that it is a mistake to insist that the Gospel has an objective substance that must somehow be translated afresh. Christianity is not a system of doctrine with an unchanging core, nor does it imply or depend on any theory of the nature of the universe, nor even on belief in a transcendent God. It can in fact, some go so far as to say, now dispense with the God-concept altogether. Christians should no longer talk in those terms. Instead, they should 'talk about man's need for a way of life or integration of personality. The words and deeds of Jesus are the gospel, the good news, because they enable men to see themselves better and live better lives. The whole supernaturalistic framework is, it is implied, as outmoded as the mythology of first century Judaism.'[1] In other words, when Christians come to understand their faith, they will recognize that it is an individual, subjective vision of the kind of life worth living, which they derive from Jesus, and which gives them insight and courage to encounter whatever comes to them day by day in their personal experience and their personal relations. They do not need, and they are not given, the security of a reasonable general outlook which can be commended to others on reasonable grounds as the objective truth.

Mr Root quotes a passage from *God Is No More* by Werner and Lotte Pelz, to illustrate this point of view:

> There is no possibility for man to find the 'truth' that is assured and will assure him—though this is precisely what we have always wanted to find. Life, by its very nature, is insecure—so is love, joy, hope—and whoever wants to accept life fully, must accept its insecurity. Not to do this means to

[1] See Root, *loc. cit.*

fall into an even greater illusion, namely that of believing that we can dispel illusions, go beyond ourselves, beyond life, that we can judge, 'become gods'.

'I can imagine', Root says, 'that in the next decade or two this new "subjectivism" *might* sweep across British theology in much the same way that the views of Ludwig Wittgenstein swept across British philosophy in the last decade or two.' It may particularly appeal to younger theologians who are tired of or bored with the problems of history and natural theology. They would no longer have to try to cope with such perennially tough questions in philosophical theology as the grounds for belief in God or the problem of evil. Root says that this prospect makes him uneasy, but he adds:

> One sometimes feels that these new voices are in touch with deeper feelings widespread in Christendom, with a deep and inarticulate longing for liberation from all the religious and intellectual paraphernalia which have encased the gospel for centuries.

That is well said, and helps to explain the eager response which many readers gave to *Honest to God*, although it should not be supposed that Dr Robinson himself intends to go all the way with the extreme subjectivists.[1] But his book revealed to a larger public than ever before that this point of view exists among professing Christians, and not only exists but can be embraced with conviction and enthusiasm.

It connects with the revulsion against the *organization* of religion, which is no new thing but was given a fresh and moving expression in the final fragments of Dietrich Bonhoeffer's thinking. And again, Christians who accept this point of view are enabled to feel as insecure and so, para-

---

[1] Nor should Bultmann, Bonhoeffer or Tillich, upon whose teaching Dr Robinson confessedly draws to a large extent, be regarded as pure subjectivists.

doxically, as much at home in this secular, empirical, changing world as anyone else. They are no longer burdened with a sense of being in this age aliens or survivors who need still to be buttressed by archaic beliefs and ruled by traditional or collective *mores* and sheltered in the sanctuary of a stable institution. There is exhilaration in knowing that you are free and open to whatever may come, and no longer wedded to doctrines that are liable to be shaken by evidence or argument and to an ethic that is based on law instead of love.

What purports to be a rationale, or to provide a dogmatic basis, for this point of view has recently been provided by Dr Paul van Buren in his book *The Secular Meaning of the Gospel* (1963). This book is well written and evinces logical acumen. I should myself find it more persuasive if it was less cocksure (although the author does allow parenthetically that there are alternatives to his interpretation of the Gospel). It may stimulate those who believe that there *are* alternatives to state them with equal vigour and clarity. But I should say that this subjectivist version of Christianity will be more effectively communicated by means of poetry, or the poetic prose of which Werner Pelz has a mastery, than by the composition of theological or christological treatises.

It strikes me that this way of translating or reinterpreting the Gospel is curiously reminiscent of Liberal Protestantism. There is the same subjectivism and individualism and distrust of the capacity of the human mind to engage in metaphysical speculation. There is the same willingness to reduce Christianity to what is held to be the essential faith and teaching of Jesus which is contrasted with what the Church subsequently imposed upon it. It is true that Harnack and Réville, for example, retained, and attached importance to, the conception of the Fatherhood of God, though we may recall that Réville, after saying that the sovereign affirmation of the Gospel is: 'Thou shalt love the Lord thy God with all thy heart, with all thy soul, with all thy mind: thou shalt love thy neighbour as thyself', added 'And these two commandments are one and the same'.[1]

Nevertheless, theological fashions or movements do not simply repeat themselves, and if we have here Liberal Protestantism come to life again it has been reborn in a world that has lost the sense of urbane confidence and security that was possible at the beginning of the century. Its concern now is with personal existence, not with promulgating the timeless 'essence of Christianity'.

There are naturally many gradations between these two ways of translating the Gospel which I have distinguished and contrasted. It is tempting to try to classify the reputedly 'Christian Radicals' under one head or the other: but I resist the temptation both because it would be premature to yield to it and because what is apparent at present is a wide variety of individual essays in new ways of interpreting Christianity or of defending the Christian religion. Writers like Professor R. B. Braithwaite[2] and Mr John Wren-Lewis,[3] for example, obviously have some affinities with the second point of view which I have distinguished, but it would be unjust to classify them either together or with anyone else: one would be obscuring the independence of their approaches and of their conclusions, in so far as they have come to conclusions. I agree with Mr David Edwards who says:

> What has been achieved so far has been little more than a series of gestures to show that some Christians are anxious to enter into a real conversation with more typical citizens of our secular society. What is needed is not a premature theological synthesis, and even more certainly not the organization of a new religious party, but a host of other experiments in thought and life.[4]

[1] See p. 22 above.
[2] See his *An Empiricist's View of the Nature of Religious Belief* (1955). There is an affinity between his view of dogma and that of Édouard Le Roy.
[3] See his open lecture at Cambridge in the Lent Term 1964, in *Faith, Fact and Fantasy* (Collins).
[4] *The Honest to God Debate*, p. 24.

But there was a further suggestion at the end of Mr Root's article that I should like to take up (he was following a suggestion that had been made by Professor R. W. Hepburn). The suggestion is that there could be a third way of responding to the present theological situation, which would be neither insistence that somehow the alleged objective substance of the traditional Gospel must be justified nor following instead the road to thorough-going subjectivism. The third way would start from the admission that there is at present no one form of belief or unbelief that can be conclusively shown to be more reasonable or self-commending than all others. In Professor Hepburn's words, it may be 'that in the end we have a choice between two equally possible readings of an ambiguous total pattern—a sceptical reading or a theistic reading'. I would add that there may well be more than two. If that be so, the task of thinkers in this field is to make as explicit as possible what the options are so as to help people to make as fully informed a choice as possible between them. Mr Root's comment is as follows :

> Instead of beginning with the attempt to justify the objective core of the gospel, or, on the other side, by embracing a purely subjective gospel, one might begin by describing and elucidating the options, the various readings of the ambiguous total pattern. What is there to choose between a sceptical and a Christian reading? What, for that matter, is there to choose between the varieties of scepticism or the varieties of religion? If one cannot ignore the claims of logic, neither can one ignore the claims of other religions. What of the pattern seen by Hindu, Buddhist, or Muslim? Or closer at home, what about those readings given by imaginative, creative artists? . . . If the gospel is to be commended in any form, it must be commended by those with an imaginative awareness of its alternatives.

This broadly conceived and demanding task is one that should especially be undertaken or promoted by divinity faculties or departments of religious studies in liberal universities.[1] That is to say, there should be courses and lectures not only 'for the defence of the Christian religion', but also for the elucidation of the options that are open to reasonable men in this age of the world. Some of the essays in *Soundings* were written from this point of view, notably that by Professor Ninian Smart, who in his other writings has urged and illustrated the need for a dialogue of religions. I also think that the essays of Mr H. A. Williams should be seen in this context. If I understand him aright, he is seeking to show in the light of contemporary psychology that statements of religious doctrine, which look like, and have commonly been taken to be, and indeed may be statements of objective truth, may also be expounded as clues to self-understanding .This was the theme of his essay on 'Theology as Self-Awareness'. I am sure that we need many more essays of this kind, since the old way of arguing about doctrinal propositions seems to have come more or less to a deadlock. Essays of this kind will be continuing the work which some of the Roman Catholic Modernists began. We can see now that attacks on, as well as defences of, the Christian religion, if they are to get anywhere, require many more resources than skill in the use of logic.

A PERSONAL CONCLUSION

Perhaps, before I finish, I ought to say something about where I myself stand in all this. I am not eager to do so, for various reasons—though not from a reluctance to testify to my beliefs. I have done plenty of that, and probably too much, in books that I have published during the past thirty years, none of which I have withdrawn, though there may be some things in them, especially in those that appeared in the heyday of Neo-Orthodoxy, that might now embarrass me. But, as I said in my first lecture, I am more interested in other people's thoughts than in my own. I regard my proper

[1] See my essay on 'The Future of Divinity' in *Crisis in the Humanities*, edited by J. H. Plumb (1964).

role as an editorial one, or as that of a midwife to theologians, and I am content with that role.

Then, I have for long felt the force of the Coleridgean maxim that men are mostly right in what they affirm and wrong in that they deny:[1] right in what they affirm, i.e. if they are not merely being clever in argument but are trying to articulate what they have proved on their pulses or what makes them tick, if I may put it so. I have learned constantly, and I want to go on learning, from what all sorts of people affirm—not least, I may say, from the various thinkers whom I have been considering in these lectures. I believe that this is the providential method of our education.

As regards the present time, therefore, I have no disposition and no sense of obligation to come down on one side or the other: anyhow, there are too many sides. I am not myself selling out either to the objectivists or to the subjectivists, though I think there is just now more to be learned from the latter. I am sensible of the appeal of thorough-going subjectivism. Not only do I feel its attraction, but I think that it has a special suitability and justification in this interim or transitional period when we are not ripe for a new theological construction. (I know that all periods are interim or transitional, but some are more so than others!) I cannot, however, persuade myself that men will or ought to abandon the quest for objective truth, nor that the transcendent, and metaphysics, and the idea of there being two worlds, have all had their day and may without compunction be consigned to oblivion. I grant that the way we think of them needs of be renewed and even to be begun all over again, but it seems to me highly improbable that the pendulum swing of human thought has come finally to rest at the subjectivist pole.

As I am not selling out to subjectivism, I am not selling out to secularism either. I can see what is meant by the secularisation of the modern world and that it is an epoch-

[1] See S. T. Coleridge, *Biographia Literaria* (1847), i. 254; cp. *Life of F. D. Maurice* (1884), i. 127.

making kind of discovery. But I can also see that we are at present sociologically conditioned to an almost exclusive preoccupation with the secular, and for that reason—and with the past and the future in mind, not to mention the eternal —I mean to keep myself open to the possibility that more is available to human experience than is comprised within the secular perspective. Secular man is not necessarily the measure of the spiritual possibilities of the human race any more than John Bull is.

Actually—while this does not, of course, exclude other motives and convictions—what makes me tick or keeps me going as a Christian is not what other people say keeps them going. It is the whole Christian movement in history of which I am thankful to be an inheritor, into which I am grateful to have been received, which I want to see continuing, however much it needs to be further developed and enlarged, reformed or refined. That is why of all the defenders of the Christian religion whom I have considered in these lectures it is the Roman Catholic Modernists with whom I feel most kinship, not least because they could not see the end of their enterprise. I agree, for instance, with M. Loisy when he said that we ought to

> make the best of what is in view of what ought to be, to repudiate none of the heritage which the Christian centuries have transmitted to ours, to recognize the necessity and the utility of the immense development that has taken place in the Church, to reap its fruits and to continue it, because the adaptation of the gospel to the changing condition of humanity is requisite today as always and more than ever.[1]

The Christian movement in history is of course much bigger than any one church or than all the churches put together. I hope that churches in the future will be much more open and flexible and comprehensive than they have been in the past, and also less religious, though I do not think a completely 'religionless' Christianity is possible or desirable.

[1] See pp. 44f. above.

I would be both for and against the Church. I accept the words of the German theological student who said:

> We must try to be at one and the same time *for* the Church and *against* the Church. They alone can serve her faithfully whose consciences are continually exercised as to whether they ought not, for Christ's sake, to leave her.[1]

I believe that men need to belong to a concrete community which is universal in principle, and which holds them together as men (the first and the last Adam) and not merely as citizens or as members of a profession or sectional club; a community which represents and sustains a way of life and a way of thought that are traditional and deeply rooted in the past but also open to change and development as the dynamism of history moves on; a community which, while it can draw its lines tighter in times of emergency as in Germany in the 1930s, is always reluctant to do so, and which binds together people of all kinds of temperament, with great diversities of experience and opinion, of mental aptitude and inclination; a community in which conditions are provided for men to go on learning from and through one another and in which they are prevented from supposing that they ever have a monopoly of the light.

For this reason, I am glad that there are the beginnings of a promising commotion in the churches, and that windows and sluices are being opened which twenty years ago seemed to be pretty firmly closed. I find it encouraging that, though there have naturally been expressions of alarm, churches do not at present seem to be trying to suppress their radicals. May we take it that they have at last learned that, in the words of Sir Will Spens, 'if theological thought is to possess any high degree of authority, not only must such thought be closely related to experience, but the consensus of opinion must be a free consensus'?[2]

[1] See E. L. Allen, *A Guide to the Thought of Karl Barth* (1950), p. 17.
[2] See p. 74 above.

Appended Note

Anglican Modern Churchmanship

O N E O F the more glaring omissions in this course of lectures was the absence of any consideration of the Anglican Modern Churchmen, who were better known in the period between the two world wars than they are now. They certainly formed a distinguishable and a distinguished group within the Church of England. They were organized in the Modern Churchmen's Union, which was at first known as the Churchmen's Union. They had their own journal *The Modern Churchman*, and they held annual conferences each summer which sometimes received a good deal of publicity for reasons other than that they occurred during the silly season. Notably their conference at Girton College, Cambridge, in 1921 set off a controversy that led indirectly to the appointment of the Archbishops' Commission on Christian Doctrine.[1]

Some of the most erudite and formidable of English theologians were members of the Modern Churchmen's Union in its palmy days, i.e. around the 1920s: e.g. A. J. Carlyle, R. H. Charles, J. M. Creed, Percy Gardner, W. R. Inge, H. D. A. Major, Hastings Rashdall, C. E. Raven, C. J. Shebbeare and B. H. Streeter (to name only a few). But it seems to me that they were a group of highly gifted individuals without a positive common mind or any such popular following as to constitute a fashion. They were academic in both the strong and the limiting sense of that word. They held sound learning in high regard and so were

[1] Cp. p. 81 above.

against theological obscurantism. Most of them disliked Anglo-Catholicism.

Though they called themselves 'Modernists', their affinity was much more with Liberal Protestantism than with Catholic Modernism, with the exception of a few like J. F. Bethune-Baker.[1] Their doyen, W. R. Inge, was one of the most persistent critics of the Roman Modernists.[2] Anglican Modern Churchmen, however, were never so theologically radical as the pure Liberal Protestants, perhaps because they were attached to the use of the Book of Common Prayer and to the establishment of the Church of England. Politically, socially and ecclesiastically they tended to be conservative. As an organized group they never attracted me, though I learned much from them individually. I could never forget that, despite their professions of liberality, they supported E. W. Barnes when, as Bishop of Birmingham, he was pursuing a most illiberal and intolerant ecclesiastical policy in his diocese.

However, if there had been time, I should like to have included in these lectures an appreciation of their achievements and an estimate of their influence. *Modernism in the English Church* by Percy Gardner (1926) and *English Modernism: its Origin, Methods, Aims* by H. D. A. Major (1927) may be consulted, as well as the files of *The Modern Churchman*.

[1] See his book *The Way of Modernism* (1927), chapter i.
[2] E.g. see his *Outspoken Essays*, 1st series, chapter vi.

INDEX

Gardner, P., 123f.
Gore, C., 24, 26, 29, 56ff., 83f.

Halifax, Viscount, 56
Hardie, Keir, 96
Harnack, A. von, 12-20, 25-8, 38-43, 48, 56, 66, 96, 116
Hegel, G. W. F., 27
Hepburn, R. W., 118
Hibbert Journal, 103
Hitler, A., 87
Honest to God, 105-9, 111, 115
Hort, F. J. A., 111
Hoskyns, Sir E. C., 70, 90ff.
Hügel, F. von, 29, 36, 39, 47, 56, 71

Inge, W. R., 123f.

James, W., 35, 55
John XXIII, 109f.

Kierkegaard, S., 86
Kittel, G., 91
Knox, W. L., 70

Laberthonnière, L., 35, 51
Lacey, T. A., 56
Lagrange, M. J., 36
Lamennais, F., 32f., 35, 57
Le Roy, E., 35, 51-55, 58, 76, 113, 117
Leo XIII, 34ff.
Liberal Protestantism, 11-31, 60, 63-8, 74, 86, 91f., 96, 113, 116f., 123
Linguistic analysis, 103
Loisy, A., 35, 37-47, 50f., 56, 65, 121

Luther, M., 11, 86
Lux Mundi, 24, 57, 69ff.

Macquarrie, J., 10
Major, H. D. A., 123f.
Mascall, E. L., 89
Maurice, F. D., 57, 100, 120
Metaphysics, 74, 120
Modern Churchmen, 81, 123f.
Modernism, Roman Catholic, 11, 26, 32-55, 74ff., 90f., 109, 113, 119, 121, 123
More, P. E., 64

Naturalism, 62ff.
Neo-Orthodoxy, 82-101, 119
New Theology, 25-31, 103
Newman, J. H., 34, 39, 48, 57, 66f.
Niebuhr, Reinhold, 95, 99

Objections to Christian Belief, 105-8

Pantheism, 63
Parker, J., 25
Pauck, W., 17
Peabody, F., 96
Pelz, W., 106, 114, 116
Petre, M., 37, 109
Pius IX, 33f., 36, 83f.
Pius X, 36
Pragmatism, 35, 55, 76
Psychology, 27f., 50, 53, 63, 119

Quick, O. C., 65-9, 113